FRANÇOIS RABELAIS

FRANÇOIS RABELAIS

The Great Story Teller

Paul Eldridge

South Brunswick and New York: A. S. Barnes and Company
London: Thomas Yoseloff Ltd

Library of Congress Catalogue Card Number: 73-124198

A. S. Barnes and Co., Inc.
Cranbury, New Jersey 08512

Thomas Yoseloff Ltd
108 New Bond Street
London W1Y OQX, England

ISBN 0-498-07799-3
Printed in the United States of America

To

SYLVETTE

My Story Without End

CONTENTS

CONTENTS

FRANÇOIS RABELAIS

L'ENVOIE

"What is that first city of the world that you speak about?" asked Pantagruel, son of Gargantua.

"Chinon," answered François Rabelais, "or Cainon, in Touraine."

"I know that Chinon is very ancient and noble and its coat-of-arms attests it:

'Chinon, Chinon, Chinon,
Little town, great renown,
On old stone long has it stood.
There is the Vienne if you look down,
If you look up, there's the town.'"

"But how is it the *first* city of the world? Where is it written? What proof have you?"

"I have found it in the Holy Scripture, which says that Cain was the first builder of cities, and it is natural that he should give his name—*Cainon*—to the first city he built."

And this is how it came about!

1

GENESIACAL REGRETS—BROTHERHOOD —DIVINE NOSES ARE SENSITIVE— EARTH'S FIRST TOWN—FIRST TOWN'S FIRST MAN

Yahweh had created the Earth and all her treasures, and made her two lights, the greater to rule the day and the lesser the night, and as adornment He added the glittering necklace of stars.

In playful mood, He kneaded from the mud splashed by the first rain a creature resembling Himself as the trembling shadow in a wind-tossed lake resembles the object which casts it. And He called him Adam, which means Red, for He had scratched him and a thread of blood meandered across his face.

Flushed with artistic ebullience, Yahweh fashioned from Adam's fragile rib the world's fairest being. Long did He, enraptured, gaze at her whose eyes were as blue as the Firmament He had created a few days previously and whose hair tumbling over her shoulders glowed as the first sunset pouring into the River Pison which compassed the whole land of Havilah.

"Chava!" Yahweh called out. "Thou art Life!"

And all the Earth echoed: "Chava! Thou art Life!"

The sun rose and the sun sank and of the seesaw Time was born. And in time, Yahweh pondered sadly that molding the rib, He had been far more concerned with

13

the perfection of femininity than with the adequate measure and quality of the brain, and this He realized was the origin of the tragedy in the Garden of Eden and thereafter upon all the Earth and the Universe.

For countless eons He, measureless Spirit, had moved over the Void, and there was neither pain nor sorrow nor death. Why had He suddenly decided to become a creator? What had prompted Him—vanity, boredom, hankering for adulation? And to escape the Earth he was constrained to create Heaven and angels to take care of it, and devils as scapegoats for his errors. Ah, the vast and desolate folly!

But should He have forgiven the disobedience and allowed the foolish pair to continue their blissful existence in the Garden of Eden, which He had planted especially for them, and thus remove death and pain and sorrow? Why, the Universe was rooted in irrevocable and immutable obedience. But let a sparrow's feather in mid air refuse to fall and the stars would lose their anchor, the moon would shine by day and the sun would darken the face of the Earth, and the Firmament would drown in the waters which He had gathered underneath it. Why, He Himself existed by the inalterable obedience to Himself!

Adam had known Eve and in travail, as commanded, Eve gave birth to two sons, Cain and Abel. Cain, like his father, was dark-haired and black-eyed, heavy-set and powerful, and like his father, he was a tiller of the soil, humorless and taciturn. Abel, like his mother, was fair-haired and blue-eyed, tall and agile. He was a keeper of sheep and an improviser of melodies on the reed. Birds would cock their heads and answer him, and he would laugh joyously, while his brother would grumble and scold.

"You do nothing but sit on your haunches and blow into that reed, and your sheep grow fat eating of my grass."

"But you are welcome to their meat and their wool, brother," Abel answered gently.

"But to whom does our mother give the choicest morsels, and whose coat does she make with greater care?" Cain asked, his black eyes blazing, for he had inherited from his father, who had inherited from Yahweh, the bile of jealousy.

"That's only because I am younger, and all mothers take greater care of their younger children, as you can see with the sheep and the birds," Abel replied.

"When I was her only child," Cain said, "she would tell me about Eden and put me to sleep singing the songs she had heard in the Garden. But when you came, she forgot me and kept you on her lap and talked to you and sang to you. Would you had never been born!" he spat.

It was autumn in the year 3875, one hundred and twenty-nine years since the creation of the world. The sun was half-risen from the river, the cool water pouring over its sleepy red face, as the two brothers were preparing to make their first offerings to Yahweh—Cain tying sheaves of wheat and Abel choosing the firstling of his flock.

They built fires.

Abel caressed tenderly the young animal, then slashed its throat. When the blood stopped gushing, he placed the carcass on the fire, and the fragrant smoke rose straight upward as if carried on shoulders. They heard athwart the field Yahweh inhaling deeply and uttering: "Ah! Ah! Ah!" And Abel was jubilant.

Now Cain set the sheaves of wheat on his fire. The flame sputtered and the smoke, acrid and thick, meandered across the surface like snakes. And they heard Yahweh cough and sneeze. And presently the wheat was sprayed and the fire put out.

Abel burst into laughter.

"Why are you laughing?" Cain demanded.

Abel pointed to the smouldering pile.

"There was too much rain and the wheat rotted," Cain explained. "Is it my fault?"

"It is!" Yahweh's voice shook the field. Since the fall of Eden He never again showed Himself, but always made His presence known in thunder and in lightning. "Sin lies at your door, Cain!"

Exulting, Abel played a triumphant piece. The birds responded in song and the sheep bleated their innocent "meh—meh—meh—"

"Stop it! Stop playing!" Cain shouted.

Abel paid no heed.

"Stop it!" Cain warned as he lifted a rock.

Abel played on.

Cain hurled the rock at his brother's head and Abel fell, his blood mingling with the blood of the firstling he had sacrificed to Yahweh.

Cain fled, but soon the voice of Yahweh was a wall which stopped him. "Where is Abel, your brother?" the voice demanded.

"Am I my brother's keeper?"

"Every man is his brother's keeper, Cain, and he who slays his brother slays himself. Your days, therefore, shall be filled with remorse, and you shall wander long upon Earth until at last you shall find your haven."

"How shall I know my haven?" Cain asked.

"Your heart will be at peace."

Cain watched the sun set and he said to himself: "The sun sinks into the water as my heart sinks into my bowels. Therefore I shall follow the path of the sun."

And westward he went and many were the years of his wandering and of his anguish.

No one dared lay hands upon him, for they said: "He is the man who slew his brother; therefore he is strong. So let us not touch him, lest he slay us, too."

Centuries later, those who slew thousands of their brothers were called heroes and they were honored, and those who slew hundreds of thousands were called kings and they were revered. And there came those who slew millions, and one so mighty who by a pressure of his thumb half of the earth burst into flames.

And the dust of Cain called unto Yahweh: "I slew only one brother and Thou madest me a homeless wanderer, hated and shunned by all men. But they who slay brothers by the thousands and by the millions are the lords of their lands, and temples and statues are raised in their honor. Erase my name from the Book of Sin! Carve it on the Tablet of Virtue!"

But Yahweh heard not his voice, for long, long since, in fierce rage that quaked the earth, He hid Himself in the farthest corner of outer space, whence all eternity would not suffice for one ray of light to cross the universe, which He in His measureless folly had created. There with a faithful she-demon, He cultivated His garden and lived in the bliss of ignorance.

Meanwhile Cain continued his wandering westward until one day he reached a river whose pellucid waters flowed gently athwart a valley cradled by hills and forests, and he said to his wives and sons who accompanied him: "There is peace in my heart; therefore I have reached my haven. I shall build a city on this spot, the first upon earth, and it shall be named Cainon in my honor, and it shall be the finest and it shall last forever."

As the generations passed, various were the peoples that occupied Cainon—Gauls and Romans and Visigoths, and the Franks who became the French and whose liquid tongue changed the name to Chinon.

And here it was that a Maid led an army and crowned a king and saved her nation from the foreign invader, for which service she was burned at the stake.

And here it was that a man was born whose statue now stands on the river quay, and who gave the city luster and renown. And his name is François Rabelais.

2

ROOTS—FIRST BLOSSOMS

Not only is the province of Touraine, watered by the Loire and its tributaries, blessed with a soil so wonderfully fertile that it has earned the name of "the garden of France," but in its wealth it also counts some of the nation's most illustrious sons. There is Richelieu the statesman; Balzac the novelist; Descartes the philosopher, whose maxim, *"Cogito, ergo sum"* (I think, therefore I am), is the most deceptive of ironies, for if thinking were indeed the evidence of existence, the earth would almost entirely be freed from the burden of that strange ceature who in his vainglory dares call himself *Homo sapiens*.

How much truer would have been the dictum: *"Non cogito, ergo sum"*—"I do not think, therefore I am." For, if man could live by reason, what reason would there be for him to live?

And there was François Rabelais.

Antoine Rabelais, sieur de La Devinière, Licencié ès Lois, Seneschal of Lerné, advocate-general in the courts of the district of Chinon and deputy Lieutenant-General, was the son of Andrée Pavin of Angers in Anjou. At her death in the year 1505, he inherited the property, castle, and mansion of Chavigny-en-Valée in the township of Varenne-sur-Seine, together with all seignorial and manorial rights, taxes, rents, income and services, hunting, fishing and grazing.

18

How old Antoine was at the time of his mother's death is unknown, but he had already been married for some fifteen years to a member of the middle-upper-class family of Dusoul, and had received as dowry a large house in Chinon, on the Rue de la Lamproie, which a half-century later became the tavern and tennis court "At the Sign of the Lamprey," and which confused many early biographers, who believed that Antoine had been an innkeeper.

There was a cellar which pertained to this house, but to reach it, contrary to all the laws of architecture, one had to climb a tortuous staircase whose last rung stood parallel with the castle dominating the town. To enter it, one had to go through an archway covered with paintings, giving it the name of the "Painted Cellar."

Within it there were many kegs of the best wine in the world, that is, the white wine of Touraine, or so it is claimed by the natives; and no one ever left thirsty.

The trip downward was, against all the laws of gravitation, far more difficult of accomplishing than the climbing, but there is no record of any severe injury, and it would seem that the son of Zeus and Semele, god Bacchus, took good care of his worshipers.

There is, however, the account of the poet Lepole, well known in Touraine in his day, but now utterly forgotten, who wrote and published a poem in which he stated that he was certain the earth turned, for his head felt in complete harmony with it after draining a tankard in the Painted Cellar.

It was fortunate for him that the Holy Office concluded after much deliberation that being a poet he was naturally empty-headed, and therefore it turned easily, and he had the illusion and the impudence to believe that the earth turned with it. The poem was ordered burned in the town square as warning and delectation for the citizens, and its author forbidden to ever again enter the Painted Cellar, a penalty which hastened his death and the death of his memory.

Although the noble Admiral Cristóbal Colón had recently discovered "India" by going in the opposite direction, it was an unforgivable heresy to openly declare, whether in a state of sobriety or inebriation, that the earth was round and that it turned.

The logic was simple: Let the earth be only a ball turning about itself and about the sun, and what was man but an insignificant insect insecurely gripping its surface? And what, indeed, was truth but the skillful adaptation of falsehood to circumstances? Therefore it was good for man to consider the earth flat and motionless and in the center of the universe; and it was proper for the Church, man's guardian by the grace of the Almighty, to extirpate anyone who dared dispute this, together with his vile notions.

Maître Antoine owned, besides the manor house of Chavigny-en-Valée, the farm of La Devinière, situated in the parish of Saint-Pierre de Seuilly, opposite La Roche-Clermant, a league from Chinon. Here he planted the *pineau,* a small dark grape as exquisite, so the Bishop said, as the one Noah, assisted by Satan (as is well known by all scholarly theologians), cultivated after the great waters had receded and the wrath of Yahweh had been appeased.

The Bishop also claimed that it was Satan, who loved to degrade God's handiwork, who got the former skipper of the Ark drunk and nude that he might be put to shame before his sons and daughters—a poignant lesson for all men never to go into partnership with the Devil. And he further added the warning that the Horned One often assumed the shape of a woman, and that in this guise he was most cunning and most vicious, to which many a miserable husband could bear testimony.

However, with all due respect to His Reverence,

woman has always rejected the Devil's services, for she could do the job splendidly without the cumbersome masquerade, and even though he did not require the usual fee—the soul. But this may have been a ruse, and a not too subtle one, for theologians have always debated the existence of feminine souls. And it may be that the reason there is neither giving nor taking into marriage in Heaven is simply the fact that there are no female spirits among the exalted of the Lord—all males.

Madame Rabelais, wife of Maître Antoine, who had already borne three children—Antoine, Jamet, and Françoise—when no longer young, gave birth to her fourth and last on the fourth of February, 1494 (according to the latest agreement among researchers)—a male child. They christened him François, so common a name that it may be conjectured the parents were bored and considered his arrival a nuisance, undeserving of any attention.

Later, indeed, this proved to be correct, since unwilling to let François share in the family wealth, they had him entered into a religious order, thereby becoming *"civilement mort"*—legally dead.

"When there are too many children, whether male or female, in some good family, inasmuch that the house would come to nothing, if the paternal estate were shared among all, as reason requires, nature directs and God commands, parents rid themselves of their children."

When Antoine died in 1535, the family property was divided among Jamet and Antoine (Jr.), René Pallu and Françoise Rabelais, his wife, Jean Gallet and Michel Endre. Not a sou went to poor François, who had been, and would remain, in perpetual financial distress, and who had good reason often to lament: "Lack of money—there is no affliction like it."

It was not, however, at Maître Antoine's manor house at Chinon that François was born, but at La Divinière, although he would always describe himself as *Chinonensis,* a native of Chinon, and he was baptized in the Benedictine Church of Saint-Pierre de Seuilly.

La Divinière still stands—a plain, small fifteenth-century house, built of stone, with farmyards and out-buildings. The surroundings were rich in historic and legendary associations, and François recalled them tenderly in later life.

François, like Gargantua (whom he would create in due time), "from the age of three to the age of five, was brought up and instructed in all proper discipline, by order of his father; and this period he spent like all the children of the country, namely: in drinking, eating and sleeping; in eating, sleeping and drinking; in sleeping, drinking and eating. He wallowed in mud, smudged his nose, dirtied his face, ran his shoes over at the heels, frequently caught flies with his mouth and liked to chase the butterflies of his father's realms."

After the age of five and until nine or ten, François received as good an education as was possible at Chinon, and then was sent to the village of Seuilly, where there was an abbey, for further instruction, to become a monk.

The ancient monk at Seuilly meditated sadly on the subject of mothers whose children they destined from infancy to cloister. "I am amazed that they carry them for nine months beneath their hearts, seeing that in their homes they cannot bear or suffer them nine years, nor even seven, more often, and simply by adding an ell to their dress and cutting I know not how many hairs from the top of their head, by means of certain words, they turn them into monks."

But was it really François' mother who had destined him for the cloister? So little is known about her, not even her name, yet it is safe to assume that it *was* she rather than her husband, who willed it, for Antoine was not a poor man and his family was not too great. Taught by the Church that sex was a thing of shame and iniquity, the mother might have desired to offer to the Lord a pure lamb as propitiatory sacrifice for her sins.

And if the lady has been maligned by generations of biographers, it must be remembered that as long as men continue their diatribes against woman, she can afford to look upon the decay of chivalry with perfect equanamity. Their expostulation is the wind which carries her to ports of conquest.

3

GRAY FRIAR—AMBIVALENCE

*F*rançois, already something of a scholar, left Seuilly to become a novice and to obtain a higher education at La Baumette, in Angers, a Franciscan friary fifty miles north of Chinon, founded by René I.

René I (1409-1480) was Duke of Anjou and Lorraine, Count of Provence and Piedmont, King of Naples, Sicily and Jerusalem, but despite these drawbacks he painted and wrote poetry, cultivated the arts and letters, encouraged the performances of mystery plays, and founded the Order of Chivalry—*Ordre du Croissant*.

René died in July, 1480, mourned by his people for his charities, his pacific character and paternal attitude. *"Nemo ante obitum beatus est,"* says the wise Roman. "No one can be considered happy before he is dead." It may be that René, despite his many tribulations and tragedies, considered himself a happy man, for he knew, as he lay dying, that he was so beloved, he would forever be known as "Le Bon Roi René"—"The Good," of all titles the rarest among kings—and commoners.

When precisely François completed his novitiate and took the vows is uncertain, but on a document for the purchase of land by the Franciscan Order of Fontenay-le-Comte, dated April 15, 1519, his signature is appended as a *frère mineur*. Therefore, at some time before that date, François had left La Baumette and entered the monastery of Puy-Saint-Martin at Fontenay-

24

le-Comte, capital of Lower Poitou, where he was or-
dained a Gray Friar, that is a member of the Franciscan
Order, "the brethren of which took vows of ignorance
as well as religious vows."

"My sovereign Lord, think not that I have placed
him in that lousy college, which they call Montague. I
had rather have put him amongst gravediggers of Sanct
Innocent, so enormous is the cruelty and villainy I have
known there; for the galley-slaves are far better amongst
the Moors and the Tartars, the murderers in criminal
dungeons, yea, the very dogs in your house, than are the
poor wretched students in aforesaid college. And if I
were King of Paris, the devil take me if I would not set
it on fire and burn both the Principal and the Regents
for suffering this inhumanity to be exercised before their
eyes."

This redoubtable school situated in the Rue des Sept-
Voies had as its director an unsavory individual, most
fittingly named Tempête—Tempest—whose life was
dedicated to two impassioned pursuits—heresy hunting
and student flogging.

Was La Baumette or Puy-Saint-Martin another Montague? For countless generations pedagogues believed
that whipping a boy's posterior stimulated his brain and
that by feruling his knuckles stirred his blood to moral
deeds. And the religious schools added monstrous punishments to prepare him for saintliness.

The result was often duplicity and animosity.

François Rabelais harbored lifelong bitter memories
of his schooldays, of his teachers, of his colleagues. Why,
then, did he persist in his novitiate until his ordination?
He was of a rebellious nature; why did he not run away?
True, fathers at the time had formidable powers over
their progeny, being, indeed, *in loco deorum*; yet both
gods and men could be circumvented, and often were—
the gods in particular.

If it was merely renouncing his share of the family wealth, after his pater's demise, he could have obliged, or if he persisted in clamoring for his rights, Maître Antoine, the cunning lawyer, who would add many unnecessary letters to his words in order to stretch out his scrolls for additional fees, could surely have found the required loopholes in the embroidery of the law to keep his errant son's hands out of the Rabelais till.

Nor could it have been physical disability, which often seemed the reason for monastic dedication. "You give to the Lord your abortions, the worst that you have. If there is to be found among your sons and among your daughters a child that is lame, hunchbacked, blind in one eye, misshapen, crippled, that one you say will make a good priest, a monk, a nun, and you proceed to offer him or her to God, as one offers a scurvy pig to St. Anthony or a sick hen to St. Valentine."

François Rabelais never complained about his health, and his foes, in their malicious distortions of his personality, never mentioned any deformity. In one of the *Prologues,* he describes himself: "Hale and hearty, as sound as a bell, and always ready to drink, if you will." And we know his face: an aggressive nose; dark, shrewd eyes, twinkling with gentle malice; a firm, impatient mouth; brows arching in mockery or amusement."

Moreover, he doubtless had himself in mind, as he painted a scholarly monk: "Contemplate a little the form, fashion and carriage of the man. Exceeding earnestly set, upon some learned meditation, and deeply plunged therein, and you shall see all the arteries of his brain are stretched forth and bent like a string of a crossbow. Nay, in such a studiously musing person, you may espy such extravagant raptures, of one, as it were, out of himself, that all his natural faculties, for the time seem to be suspended from each other their proper charge and office, and his exterior senses to be at a stand.

In a word, you cannot otherwise choose than think that he is by an extraordinary ecstasy quite transported out of what he was, or should be."

In short, a man, well proportioned and presentable and capable of intensive study. Well, then, why did François Rabelais turn monk? To seek within their deeds the motives of men is to seek within the coils of the clock the lair of the hours.

It may well be that, an early lover of learning, François was under the impression that a monastery was a place where one could devote oneself to its pursuit freed from the base passions of men and the quotidian vexations beyond the walls.

Before long, however, he realized that he had been deceived. "In our abbey the monks never study, for fear of the mumps and lest their heads should break. Our late abbot used to say that it is a monstrous thing to see a learned monk."

The mental energies of the inmates were consumed in meretricious insolubles, such as: "Is a pig that is being driven to market held by the man or by the rope?"

Yet by now François had acquired monastic habits and viewed other possible occupations, such as the army or the law, with distrust and apprehension, and the practice of medicine, in which he was to achieve renown, he would start in maturity.

There was a decided ambivalence in Rabelais toward monks and the monastic life. No one has written more mocking, and at times more virulent things about them. "If you can conceive how an ape in a family is always mocked and provokingly incensed, you shall easily apprehend how monks are shunned by all men, both young and old. A monk—I mean one of those lazy monks—does not labor like the peasant nor guard the land as does the man-at-arms, nor heal the sick like the physician, nor preach and instruct the world like the good

Evangelical doctor and the pedagogue; he does not import good and necessary things for the commonwealth like the merchant. That is the reason why by all men they are hooted at and abhorred. They disturb the whole neighborhood with the jangling of their bells. They mumble a great store of legends and psalms in no ways understood by them. They count a number of Paternosters, interlarded with long Ave Marias, without thinking or understanding them. Truly, truly, this rascally monastic vermin all over the world mind nothing but their guts and are as ravenous as any kites."

And yet whom does François Rabelais make the most vital character in his universal comedy; whom does he endow with the most kindness and active virtue (as well as with the weaknesses of men), but a monk, a real monk, "a right monk, if ever there was any since the monking world monked a monkerie," whom, but our good Friar John—Frère Jean de Entommeurs?

"Therefore everyone wishes him for his company. He is no bigot; he is not a tatterdemalion; he is honest, merry, resolute, and a good companion; he works, he labors, he defends the oppressed; he comforts the afflicted; he succors the distressed; he guards the abbey-close."

Friar John is not a literary character; he has not stepped out of books, but out of life, and of course, he is Frère François Rabelais in *propria persona*. For all portraits are self-portraits, all biographies are autobiographies, and all roads lead to our own backyard.

4

DE PROFUNDIS—OF FOXES
AND EELS—FRIENDSHIP

*I*n an ancient and forgotten cemetery in the city of Lyons there lies flat on the ground a tombstone, frail and yellow as the leaves which cover it. If one looks intently at it one can decipher the inscription carved into it:

PASSANT
Ce qui tu donnes à Dieu tu voles à l'Homme
PASSER-BY
Whatever you give to God you rob of Man

There is also the date: *Mai 5, 1488* and two letters of the original name—*p* . . . *e* . . . .

How the stone survived the merciless elements is as much a mystery, or a miracle (if one is inclined toward mysticism), as how when it was first raised it escaped the merciless hammers of the clerical authorities.

True, Lyons at the time was more tolerant toward Humanistic ideas than Paris, where the Sorbonne, the myriad-eyed Ogre, was ever ready to pounce upon men and books and devour them.

Yet the inscription was an uncompromising challenge not only to men directly employed by God but even to many humanists who harbored deistic ideas, although all were critical of the dogmas and the transgressing ways of the rulers at Rome. It was, indeed, not only utterly

29

atheistic but it also implied disgraceful traffickings in the marketplaces of the Lord.

Who was this wily $p \ldots e \ldots$, who not only escaped the flames, but even managed to be buried in holy ground and have a fine stone (for it showed signs of excellent sculpting with many embellishments) erected over his remains? Did he belong to that fraternity of the subtle "cowards" like Desiderius Erasmus and Friar François Rabelais, who, ever the jester, said: "I am by nature sufficiently thirsty without becoming more heated. I have a dread of being burned alive like a red herring, and would maintain my opinions to the fire exclusively," and who skilled in the ways of the fox and the eel succeeded in terminating their mortal days with their skins unscorched and their bones unbroken? Did he realize that ideas must always be treated with a certain degree of irony, and never be allowed to ride roughshod over him who holds them, and that the crown of martyrdom over a hollowed skull is a gesture of obscenity?

Alas, we shall never know who this $p \ldots e \ldots$ was, but we salute his ashes for the maxim he has bequeathed us, even if we should dispute its absolute validity, for a maxim is but a gadfly to prick us into thinking, not to exhaust an idea. Indeed, not all the words in the vocabulary of man can surround one idea and conquer it utterly.

At La Baumette, young François had the good fortune to make the friendship of Geoffroy d'Estissac, offspring of an ancient Touraine family, who at twenty-three became Bishop of Maillezais, where he led the fashionable life of a Renaissance lord, transformed the monastery into a palace in the Italian style, with charming cloisters, a splashing fountain, and broad, noble stairways, and planted gardens of flowers and plants.

There were also two brothers of the distinguished Du Bellay family. Jean du Bellay (1492-1560) had enlightened ideas and was a constant and liberal patron of arts, letters, and learning. While still quite young, he astounded the University of Paris by the extent of his learning, both sacred and profane. Trained in the art of dialectical debate, he held his own against the most obstinate theologians, whose innocent words were traps and whose simple questions were intricate labyrinths.

Guillaume du Bellay (1491-1543), Seigneur de Langey, soldier, diplomatist and scholar, was one of the ablest men in the kingdom.

More than once did these good men and others save Friar François, whose humor was broad and barbed, from the claws of the "hobgoblins" and the tongues of their fires.

Rabelais was ever the welcome guest in the households of the powerful and the influential. He was learned and witty, a brilliant conversationalist, and a lover of the wines of life—the intellectual and the physical. Sought after and protected by the patrons of the arts, the friends of the humanities, the masters of graceful living, François escaped the dreaded consequences of those who dared anger the hierarchy.

But he was neither a sycophant nor an ingrate. "Never did man do me a good turn but I returned it or at least acknowledged it. No, I scorn the ungrateful. I never was, nor ever will be."

And there was the other side of the coin. "Never did man do me an ill one, without ruing the day that he did it, both in this world and in the next. I am not so much of a fool either."

Where was his Christian teaching requiring the turning of the cheek? Did he consider it the cynical dictum of the tyrant who wished to enslave man, since he who turned his cheek was certain to have both slapped, or merely a locution belonging to the sacerdotal arsenal of pious words—words whose seeds blossomed into gigantic trees under whose soothing shadows men sought refuge from the consuming sun of reality?

Words, Rabelais knew, devoured the ideas which had

given them birth, and nothing remained save empty sounds to whom the credulous and the hypocrite bent knee.

Words were roaring lions, and he, François Rabelais, was the mighty tamer who made them turn as on a merry-go-round to the snap of his whip and purr at his feet like kittens. Never would he allow them to lacerate his mind. He was their master and they must do him homage, but he was a good master who tended them with affection and solicitude.

The Greek tongue—key to the treasury of poetry, art, letters, science, perfect laws, heroic virtues, stirring eloquence. For centuries Western man had wandered in the tenebrous forests of delusion, doubt and folly, but now— now he had finally discovered the wondrous cache.

Was it reasonable to expect all that mankind had ever accomplished, all the goodness and the wisdom, the truth and the beauty, to have lodged in the little islands of the Aegean Sea, two millennia ago?

What really mattered was that man would make the effort to understand that magic world. And that effort would liberate his soul. The ancient thought would stimulate his own thought, and the ancient arts would inspire his own genius. And this would be his rebirth, the Renaissance!

It was after the fall of Constantinople to the Ottoman Turks in 1453 that the precious fragments of the Hellenic treasure began to appear in the West, but not until 1495, when Janus Lascaris (1445-1535), the learned Greek, came to France, that the study of the language took root there.

At Fontenay-le-Comte, François had as his classmate Pierre Amy, who had also been one of the signatories of the document for the purchase of the land for the monastery. Some years older than François, Pierre had already been so far advanced in the study of Greek that he had acquired the esteem of some of the most famous humanists with whom he was in correspondence.

As his pupil, François made much progress and became a distinguished master of Greek literature. He was, indeed, among other notable things, a linguist of no mean attainments.

At this time, about the year 1520, the study of Greek was attended with many difficulties. There were few manuscripts, and books had to be imported from Italy. The first Greek book printed in France appeared as late as 1507, and for the next fifteen years barely averaged one a year.

Printing in general, however, grew rapidly, and Paris, which had its first press under Louis XI (1423-1483), whose father was crowned by Joan of Arc, in a cellar of the Sorbonne, and very soon had more than twenty. Lyons, center of learning, had fifty at the beginning of the sixteenth century, while Germany had already more than one thousand. Virgil was printed in 1470; Homer in 1488; Aristotle in 1498; Plato in 1512.

Pierre Amy was in correspondence with Budé. Guillaume Budé (Budaeus) (1467-1540), was born in Paris and went to the University of Orleans to study law. But for several years, being a young man of means, he led an idle and dissipated life. At the age of twenty-four, however, he was suddenly seized with remorse. Instead of turning monk, as so often was the case with those who sought divine remission of sins, Budé plunged into study, and made such progress in the Latin and Greek languages that he knew them better than anybody else in France. He gained great reputation as scholar and was secretary to the King, by whom he was held in high esteem.

Francis I (1494-1547), combined furious gallantry with pompous boasting in a typical Gallic manner. In spite of a very long and large nose, he was extremely handsome, a sturdy and valiant knight, a brilliant talker and a facile poet. His elegant clothes studded with jewels and stiff gold embroideries dazzled his people and blinded them to his grave faults. They allowed him to become more imperious and absolute, and his government was *"du bon plaisir"* (at his pleasure).

At Pavia, on February 25, 1525, he led his army to disaster, and he wrote to his mother, Louise of Savoy: "Of all things nothing remains me save honor and life, which is safe." This gave birth to the legend that he wrote the celebrated sentence: *"Tout est perdu sauve l'honneur"* (All is lost save honor).

Budé and Jean du Bellay, Bishop of Narbonne, persuaded Francis to found the Collège de France and the Library of Fontainebleau, which was later removed to Paris and was the origin of the great Bibliothèque Nationale. And this remains the King's glory.

Budé wrote learned letters in Latin and Greek to Pierre Amy at Fontenay-le-Comte, and in each he had something for Rabelais. "My salutations to your brother in religion and science. Farewell and a fourfold salutation in my name to the gentle and learned Rabelais, by word of mouth, if he is with you, or in writing if he is not."

Budé's request that he should be buried at night, and his widow's open profession of Protestantism at Geneva, where she retired after his death, caused him to be suspected of leanings toward Calvinism. At the time of the massacre of St. Bartholomew, the members of his family were obliged to flee from France.

5

BATTLE FOR GREECE—DEUS VERSUS HOMO—DAISIES—GRAY INTO BLACK— GREEN FRUIT

*I*n 1517 Martin Luther tacked up his theses in the church door of Wittenberg, and on December 10, 1521, he made a bonfire of the Canon Law—*Exurge Domine*. The Reformation was on—a revolt against the international State represented by the Medieval Church; a revolt on the part of the governments of Europe against the Papal monarchy.

In the Spring of that same year, the Sorbonne formally condemned Luther's writings, which for the last two years "had been eagerly read at Paris by the whole band of the learned," who formed a state within a state, the Republic of Letters.

Three years later, Desiderius Erasmus published his "Commentaries" on the Greek text of St. Luke and deepened the cleavage between the theologians and the humanists, while the complete break took place with the appearance of his masterpiece, *Moriae Encomium—In Praise of Folly*—whose wit and irony struck as a mighty ax at the foundations of the institutions of monasticism and priestcraft.

There was the stench of burning human flesh in Christendom, which according to the theologians delighted the Lord. A myriad varieties of sacrifices had been offered Him on the countless altars since Abel and Cain, of sacred memory, first brought theirs, and now only the smoke rising from burning men could still tickle His divine nostrils, so the learned doctors claimed. Gods die; priests remain.

Heretics pullulated and the French theologians were in urgent need of an easily identifiable scapegoat. The Calvinists were in Switzerland and the Lutherans in Germany, and therefore untouchable. (They would take care of their own heretics in due time.) In France, however, there were those who called themselves Humanists. Their very appellation was a taunt and a blasphemy. What could it mean but that they held man in higher esteem than God; that the earth was more precious to them than Heaven; that human nature was not forever evil by reason of the Original Sin, but that it tended to good and perfection? What did it mean but that the chain that bound man to the Holy Church and her holy servitors was to be broken, and he was to wander free?

And was not freedom the most perilous of sins, containing within its texture the roots of all the others? Freedom was a sword and one could never tell into which sacred bowels it would be plunged. It were far better for man to vanish from the earth than be free, and the canker must be torn out of his mind before it corrupted him utterly!

The Humanist said: "Those who are free born and well born, well brought up and used to decent society, possess by nature a certain instinct and spur which impels them to virtuous deeds and restrains them from vice, an instinct which is the thing called honor."

The maxim of Humanism was: "Live according to Nature, which is liberty as against the tyranny of the Church, whether Catholic or Protestant." To François Rabelais the fasting of Rome and the strict discipline of Geneva were equally violations of Nature and the approving of *Antiphysis*—anti-Nature. "God did not create Lent."

Where was the source of this evil called Humanism if not where its followers themselves indicated it—the poisoned waters of Greece—her tongue and her writings? Every tatter of a manuscript smuggled from Italy and Turkey was infected and should be destroyed, if possible, or at least hidden from the eyes of students, and the Sorbonne put a ban on the study of the Greek language in France.

At Fontenay-le-Comte François Rabelais and Pierre Amy, devotees of *"bonnes lettres,"* continued their study of Greek surreptitiously and even managed to collect a small classical library. But the monks who were faithful to their "vow of ignorance," became suspicious, and began whispering that the two "Hellenists" were heretics. One of them, by the name of Arthus Coultant, was particularly incensed at Rabelais. Spy and calumniator, he spread malicious lies about "trailing his monk's robe over the hedges," that is, devoting himself to drinking and debauchery, while residing within the convent walls.

Finally the chapter made a thorough search in the cells of the two monks, discovered the books, which included some by Erasmus, confiscated them, and placed Amy and Rabelais in solitary confinement. They suffered great privations and woes and feared the worst at the hands of the raging friars, which could include excommunication, anathema, torture and slow fire.

Even as Protestants, in doubts and difficulties, had the custom of opening the Holy Bible to see the divination, so these two young scholars used the *Sotes Virgilianae*— (the Virgilian Lots). And as they opened the book they found the verse: *"Heu! fuge crudeles terras! fuge littus avarum!"* (Alas! Flee this cruel land! Flee the avaricious shore!).

They obeyed the great Roman poet's recommendation, fled from "the ambuscade of the Goblins," and safe and sound, found haven in the countryside, where they had friends.

They invoked help, and Guillaume Budé and Geoffroy d'Estissac, exerting their great influence had their books returned, and they escaped physical violence.

Budé wrote them: "Your tribulations will cease, since your persecutors discovered that they were placing themselves in hostility to people of credit and to the King himself. Thus you have honorably emerged from this trial, and will, I hope, resume your work with renewed ardor."

This matter of royal intervention was not a vain boast. If the Monarch himself was not interested, then it must have been his sister, two years his senior, Marguerite d'Angoulême (1492-1549). The most celebrated of the Marguerites, she bore no less than four surnames, but as the daughter of Charles d'Orleans, count d'Angoulême, she is most properly called Marguerite d'Angoulême and Queen of Navarre.

With the accession of her brother, Francis I, to the throne, she became the most powerful woman of the kingdom. At Nérac and Pau there were miniature courts over which she held sway, and which yielded to none in Europe in intellectual brilliance of their frequenters. Marguerite, indeed, was the chief patroness of letters and of feminism in France, as well as the defender of the advocates of the Reformation, and their refuge.

Bigotry and the desire to tarnish the reputation of women of letters brought odious accusations against Marguerite's character, for which there is not the least foundation of truth. Nor did she escape the wrath of the Sorbonne for her book *Le Miroir de l'Âme Pécheresse* (The Mirror of the Sinful Soul), a pious edifying and reverent book, but not in the manner of the University. She was denounced, insulted, threatened with the gallows and the stake and ignominiously represented on the stage of the Collège de Navarre.

The Sorbonne, that is, the Faculties of Theology of the University of Paris, was founded by Robert de Sorbon (1201-1274), chaplain and confessor to Louis IX (1214-1270), known as Saint Louis.

Saint Louis stands in history as the ideal king of the Middle Ages. An accomplished knight, physically strong in spite of his ascetic practices, fearless in battle, heroic in adversity, of imperious temperament, unyielding when sure of the justness of his cause, energetic and firm, he was indeed "every inch a king." He fasted much, loved sermons, heard two Masses a day and all the offices, dressing at midnight for matins in his chapel, and surrounded even when he traveled by priests on horseback chanting the hours. After his return from the first Crusade, he wore only gray woolens in winter, dark silks in summer. He built hospitals, visited and tended the sick himself, gave charity to over a hundred beggars a day. Yet he safeguarded the royal dignity by bringing them in at the back door of the palace, and by a courtly display greater than ever before in France. He had no favorite, nor prime minister. He introduced the pontifical inquisition, and was canonized in 1297.

Sorbon's object in founding the University was to facilitate the theological studies to the poor students, designated as *Domus magistrorum pauperrimo* (Most poor house of masters).

Later the decision of the doctors of the Sorbonne enjoyed great authority in the matter of the Faith. It demanded the condemnation of Joan of Arc; it was the center of persecution of Protestants and unbelievers; it justified the massacre of St. Bartholomew; it functioned as uncompromising censor of books, which proved one of the gravest danger to letters.

With the passing of the centuries, however, the Sorbonne became one of the great centers of learning and freedom, and abolished its Faculties of Theology.

By her first husband, Marguerite had no children, by her second a son, who died in infancy, and a daughter, Jeanne d'Albret, who became the mother of Henry IV. She died on September 21, 1549, at Odot-en-Bigorre.

Although the poets of her day were unwearied in celebrating her charms, from the portraits which exist she does not seem to have been beautiful. As to her sweetness of disposition and strength of mind, there is universal consent.

Marguerite's chief literary work consists of the *Heptaméron,* of poems, entitled *Les Marguerites de la Marguerite des Princesses* (The Daisies of the Daisy of Princesses), and of *Letters.*

The *Heptaméron,* constructed, as its name indicates, on the lines of the *Decameron* of Boccaccio, consists of seventy-two delightful stories, told to one another by a company of ladies and gentlemen, who are stopped on their journey homeward by the swelling of a river. From internal evidence several of them were composed by admiring authors who fluttered about the Queen.

The *Heptaméron,* however, was not published until 1558, ten years after her death, and then under the title of *Les Amants Fortunés,* her exalted rank evidently bearing no urgency with publishers.

The *Letters* are interesting; the *Marguerites* are devotional poems and miscellaneous songs. They are good enough, considering that they come from the pen of a queen, for in the history of letters poetic genius among royalty has been conspicuous by its absence, with the possible exception of King Solomon of Palestine. And yet the Song of Songs is very likely ghost-written, since it is the glorification of one woman, while the great son of David had a vast stable of them for immediate service.

Under such circumstances a man may write a colossal farce or a horrendous tragedy, for he may be so weary of them as to order them cast to the crocodiles, but not a rapturous lyric. The real writer must have been a slave gazing longingly at the locked door of the harem, even as Dante Alighieri gazed longingly at the golden portals of Heaven behind which dwelt gentle Beatrice. The inaccessible only may inspire great poetry, and the true bard is the fisherman who throws his net to capture the horizon.

Pierre Amy took refuge in a Benedictine monastery at Saint-Mesmi, since the Benedictines, as an exception among monks, were interested in scholarship, and if they did not encourage the study of Greek, at least they did not consider it a sign of heresy. History records nothing more of Amy save that he later made his way to Switzerland and became a Lutheran, and he who has no history is generally moderately happy, and death overtakes him kindly.

Such was not the case with other friends of François Rabelais. Louis Berquin, noted for his learning and noble character, was burned for heresy. Etienne Dolet, scholar and publisher, was tortured, hanged and burned, charged with having denied the immortality of the soul in his study of Plato. Jean de Caturce de Limoux, professor of Law at the University of Toulouse, who at a state banquet made certain remarks which caused him to be suspected of Lutheranism, was burned alive in Place Saint-Etienne. History recorded *them,* and history is a long cry and the incredible account of how man, despite his monstrous follies and cruelties, has survived.

François Rabelais, less impulsive than his friend Amy, acted with greater prudence. By the help of one of his best patrons, Geoffroy d'Estissac, Bishop of Maillezais, Abbot of Saint-Pierre, Prior of Liguĝé, he succeeded in obtaining from the new Pope, Clement VII, an "indult," licensing him to become a Benedictine and to substitute the gray habit for the black, with the title of regular Canon and the right to hold benefices.

In the abbey church of Maillezais, Rabelais swore allegiance to his new Superior, Geoffroy d'Estissac, but although a nominal inmate of that abbey, he resided with his Bishop at his priory of Ligugé, near Poitiers. There the Bishop had built himself a princely château, surrounded by splendid gardens.

D'Estissac took Rabelais into service as domestic chaplain and gave him a chamber to himself at the top of a little tower, still called by his name. With books around him and peace in his heart, he translated Herodotus, "Father of History" (484-425 B.C.) into Latin.

Here Rabelais made the friendship of Jean Bouchet, native of Poitou, like himself, and author of "Annales d'Aquitaine," who also resided at the priory. He was a lawyer, scholar and philosopher, simple, dependable and kindly, a treasure of a man, who had a profound influence upon Rabelais, and was the source of his wise maxim: *"Non in malevolam animam introibit sapientia"* —"Into a malicious soul wisdom enters not."

As avocation, Jean Bouchet produced reams of verse of a mediocre quality, but in French. He urged François to also try his hand at writing in that tongue despised by Humanists and scholars, who used Latin mixed with Greek. Rabelais took his advice and indulged in "exchanging letters" in verse, the vogue of the day. The output was only slightly better than his mentor's, but resulted in his first published book, entitled *Epistles to Bouchet*.

One of his choice pieces was "a prayer."

> *O Dieu, père paterne,*
> *Qui maus l'eau en vin,*
> *Fais de mon cul lanterne*
> *Pour luyre à mon voisin.*

(O God, thou holy sire divine,
Who out of water made the wine,
Make of my arse a lantern bright
To guide my neighbor through the night.)

Already the irreverent and broad humor is in evidence. The time would come when, discarding the metric form, Rabelais would write his incomparable prose, laying the foundation for the great works of his successors, who molded the French tongue into a magnificent instrument of beauty and precision, which led to the saying: *"Ce qui n'est pas clair, n'est pas français—"* ("What is not clear is not French") until barbarous foreign influences flowed into the pellucid stream and muddied it. And the saying no longer held. Whether another François Rabelais will appear who, by his genius, will purify it again, is a matter of the future, and the future is man's creation of despair.

The great esteem in which Bouchet held Rabelais is evident in one of his "Epistles" to his friend, describing the intellectual and social life at the château of Bishop Geoffroy d'Estissac.

> *A ce moien il ayme gens lettrez*
> *En Grec, Latin, et François, bien estrez*
> *A diviser d'histoire ou theologie*
> *Dont tu es l'un, car en toute clergie*
> *Tu es expert, a ce moien te print*
> *Pour le servir, dont tresgrant heur te vint,*
> *Tu ne pouis trouver meilleur service*
> *Pour te pourveoir bien tost de benefice.*

(He [d'Estissac] likes those who are versed in Greek, Latin and French literature, and who are well equipped to converse on history or theology; of whom you are just the one, for you are skilled in all learning; and it is for this reason that he has chosen you to serve him, which is a great good luck for you seeing that you could not find employment better fitted to provide you speedily with a living.)

6

WANDERER—HIPPOCRATES AND GALEN —FRANCISCUS RABELAESUS, MEDICUS —THE LIVING ENCYCLOPEDIA

*M*an is an impatient traveler without destination. In the days of François Rabelais the world was in a tumultuous agitation. A few years previously three small sailboats captained by a man born in Italy, in the service of Spain, of probable Jewish antecedence, crossed the mysterious, devil-infested Atlantic. Almost immediately thereafter sailors began encircling the globe, discovering new lands, new seas, new rivers, while across the old continent men rushed in all directions, and like bees brimming with the pollen of the New Learning, fecundated the minds. It was a veritable explosion of tourism without the need of passports or visas, and the cultured feeling everywhere at home, since Latin was the *lingua franca*—their current tongue. Save that the rapacious theologians, eagle-eyed, hovering over all the lands, swooped upon the unwary and the reckless. Few indeed tore themselves free from their gory talons.

François Rabelais, true son of the Renaissance, was kindled with the wanderlust. He disappeared for months and even years at a time, vagabonding, his eyes and ears ever wide open to nature and her ways, and to man and his ways, studying at universities, writing, or hiding from the "Goblins" of the monasteries and the Sorbonne, whose sharp noses every time he published anything, however innocent and even infantile in its humor, sniffed sulphur underneath, and would gladly have hurled its author into the flames whence it rose.

Poitiers is only five miles distant from Ligugé and its university founded by Charles VII in 1432 during the English occupation of Paris, and had a considerable reputation, in particular its law schools with its 4,000 students, who were the best dancers of France, dancing being to scholarship what headache is to thinking.

Situated in a commanding position and surrounded by the River Clain and its tributary Boivre, Poitiers was during the Middle Ages one of the largest and strongest cities of France and the spot where Charles Martel crushed the Arabs in 732, thus freeing France and Western Europe from the Mohammedan incursion.

It was a pity, nevertheless, since for several centuries following their defeat, the Arab world to the south was one of enlightenment, while the Christian passed through a long, dark tunnel of superstition and ignorance.

François Rabelais, who considered Poitiers the peer of Lyons in cultural activities, was probably a student at the university, for his intimate acquaintance of the place and the entire upper Poitou indicated a long sojourn, which also permitted proficiency in dancing and the juggling of the two-handed sword.

Moreover, only a thorough student of legal lore could venture to write authoritatively about the Book of Laws which "impressed him as being a handsome robe of State, and an enormously precious one, but one, nevertheless, embroidered with mire, and so befouled, so infamous, and so infectious that there is nothing in it but ordure and vileness."

Rabelais probably also took courses in civil law at the University of Orleans, a swanky university town. There he wrote a doggerel for one of its graduates:

A tennis-ball in your belly-band
And a racquet in your hand;
A law book in your doctor's hood;
Scrape your feet, and scrape them good;
And you're a doctor, understand.

Orleans was famous for its tennis courts, and at the beginning of the sixteenth century had forty of them. Clerics and students were ardent enthusiasts of the sport, but whether Rabelais indulged in it is not recorded.

It was the year 1528 and François Rabelais, thirty-four years old, had made the tour of several universities. He had garnered carloads of knowledge, which with more added in time would gain him the appellation of the "living encyclopedia." By sheer force of mind and by long and arduous labors, Maître Rabelais was an "abysm of learning, the Pliny of his day."

Pliny the Elder (23-79) wrote the *Natural History* in thirty-seven books, compiled from notes filling 2,000 volumes. He commanded the fleet at Misenum and went to Stabiae to rescue the inhabitants threatened by the eruption of Vesuvius, and also to observe the phenomenon, but he arrived at the moment of the catastrophe which engulfed Herculaneum and Pompey and perished in A.D. 79, the deleterious vapors of the volcano asphyxiating him.

Pliny the Younger (61-113), his nephew and heir, writes in a letter: "My uncle began to work long before daybreak. He read nothing without making extracts. He used even to say that there was no book so bad as not to contain something of value. In the country it was only the time when he was actually in his bath that was exempted from study. In short, he decried all time wasted that was not employed to study."

"François Rabelais had achieved that polymathy which few men have possessed. It is certain that he was a learned Humanist and a very profound philosopher, theologian, mathematician, physician, jurisconsult, musician, arithmetician, geometer, astronomer, and even a painter and a poet, and all of these at one and at the same time." So says Guillaume Colletet (1598-1659), French poet, who was near enough to Rabelais' day to have met some old-timers who had known him personally and who could relate their impressions of him. But his learning was not only from books but from nature; not only literary but intellectual; not only verbal but factual and living. And, of course, it must be added that he was also, and chiefly, one of the world's great storytellers.

François Rabelais, *"in mezzo del camin de nostra vita"* (in the middle of the road of our life), as Dante considered the age of man, stood irresolute. He had been a Franciscan and turned Benedictine, but he was also a Humanist and the monastic existence angered and bored him, while the endless ringing of the bells, calling to meaningless prayers and silly duties, shattered his nerves, as the Cathedral bells would annoy the eighteenth-century philosophers. Yet, he could not, even if it had not been so perilous, shed his habit. Whatever else he might be, he was also a man of the Church. Not only his early training, but something in his nature bound him to her, and always somewhere in his heart he had an altar before which he would kneel.

Even as he would maintain his opinion "to the fire exclusive," so he would maintain his disbelief to the face of God "exclusive." Moreover, the uniform gave status, however much it was criticized, however much he himself ridiculed it. And there was always the matter of a "living," which might be forthcoming and afford him independence.

Now Destiny began to pull François Rabelais in the direction she had decided for him, and in the summer of 1528, without asking permission of his Superior, he left for Paris. It was not, to be sure, a gesture of disrespect to Bishop Geoffroy d'Estissac, but he probably did not wish to embarrass his good patron, who could not officially allow him to leave his post except on urgent matters of the Church.

In Paris Rabelais matriculated as a student of medicine, and on December 1, 1530, after two and a half years of study, was admitted to the degree of Bachelor of Medicine. As a candidate for the license, he was required to give a course of lectures.

The subjects assigned to him were the *Aphorisms* of Hippocrates and the *Ars Parva*—The Little Art—of Galen. Hitherto lecturers used Latin translations without referring to the original language. Rabelais, however, had "a very ancient" Greek manuscript of Hippocrates in his possession, and he made textual criticism a special feature of his lectures, which was something of a sensation at the University, and filled his classes with students.

His copy of Galen's complete works in four volumes, printed in Venice in 1525, with his autograph on the title page of each volume, is in the library of the University College, Sheffield. Since Rabelais had rarely any more money than needed for the day's expenses, the books, which must have been quite expensive, were surely the gift of one of his patrons, who, had he but guessed the whimsicalities of time, would have insured the immortality of his name and the eternal gratitude of scholars by signing them himself.

Hippocrates, the "Father of Medicine," was born in Cos in the first year of the 80th Olympiad, that is 460 B.C. It was claimed that he was descended from Hercules through his mother, Phaenarte. He studied medicine under his father, Heraclides, and philosophy under Democritus of Abdera. He traveled, taught and practiced his profession at Athens, and died at Larissa in Thessaly, his age being variously given as 85, 90, 104 and 109.

He was held in veneration by the Athenians, and the whole tone of his works bespeaks a man of the highest integrity and purest morality.

Although born of a family of priest-physicians and inheriting all its traditions and prejudices, Hippocrates was the first to cast superstition aside and base the practice of medicine on the principles of inductive philosophy. He was also the first to disassociate medicine from priestcraft and to direct exclusive attention to the natural history of disease. He revolted against the use of charms, amulets, incantations, and was a very careful clinical physician, placing great dependence on diet and regimen, and the reasons given by him are valid to this day, including the principles of public health.

Galen Claudius, the most celebrated of the ancient medical writers, was born at Pergamum, in Mysia, Asia Minor, about A.D. 130. He went to Rome, where he healed many persons of distinction. Because of his great learning and unparalleled success as physician, he earned the title of *"Paradoxologus"* (Wonder-Speaker) and of *"Paradoxopoeus"* (Wonder-Worker), thereby incurring the envy and jealousy of his fellow-practitioners. He died in the year 200, at the age of seventy, according to some at the age of eighty, in Sicily, where he probably sought refuge from the maliciousness of his colleagues.

Galen was one of the most versatile and accomplished writers of his age, reputed to have composed nearly 500 treatises on various subjects, including logic, ethics, and grammar, antedating by a millennium and a half the ideal of the Renaissance—universality of knowledge and the uniqueness of the individual, which some centuries later would be discarded for minute specialization and uniformity.

Yet, inevitably, Galen was also a man of his own time with its peculiar superstitions and prejudices. He was a champion of teleology, that is, Nature having designed each thing to serve a specific purpose, and thereby made of man a perfectly harmonious entity. To what ludicrous conclusions such a theory might lead is evident by Galen's dictum: "The head is made for the sake of the eyes." An enterprising optician might with equal justice say: "The nose is made for the purpose of holding spectacles."

Yet Nature has no design for man. She is neither kind to him nor cruel, and is unaware of his presence except as one of the particles in her vast totality, to be perpetuated or obliterated by the pressure and reshaping of space.

Now François Rabelais knew what he wanted—to be a doctor—a full-fledged doctor, but the studies at the University of Paris were inadequate. He decided, therefore, to pursue them at the School of Medicine at Montpellier, center of medical science for all of France and celebrated for its privileges and its doctrines. In the year 1141 Montpellier acquired a charter for its Medical School, and through the years many of its most prominent professors were Jews, who had been chiefly responsible for its founding, and who had established an important colony there. For this service they were decimated and expelled from the kingdom, and again as on so many occasions before and after, they learned that in Christendom there would never be security for the Jew.

Rabelais inscribed his name on the registry of the School of Medicine: "I, François Rabelais, of Chinon, in the diocese of Tours, have come hither for the purpose of studying medicine, and have taken as my sponsor the illustrious Master Jean Schyron, Doctor and Regents of the University. I promise to observe all the statutes of the said School of Medicine which are usually kept by those who have in good faith signed their name and taken the oath, according to custom, and to this I have set my signature with my own hand, this 17th day of September, in the year of Our Lord, 1530."

And on the margin is written: "Biij," an abbreviation for *solvit tres libras*—paid three livres—the matriculation fee consisting of two livres for the right to become a scholar and one livre for the proctor.

Rabelais was an excellent student and acquired a profound knowledge of anatomy and botany, but left the school in 1532 without obtaining his degree, although he had already practiced and unofficially called himself Maître François Rabelais, Doctor of Medicine.

In 1537, however, he did receive his degree, and was invested with the insignia proper to a Doctor of Medicine—a gold ring, a gilt belt, a black cloth biretta surmounted with a crimson silk tassel, and a copy of Hippocrates.

The conferring of the doctorate at Montpellier was a colorful affair. After six examinations lasting three days, the candidate receiving two-thirds vote was ready for the *actus triumphalis*. The ceremony took place in the Church of Saint-Firmin, and was heralded the evening before by the ringing of the great bell. There were academic processions, Latin addresses and the presentation of the diploma. After which, the newly created doctor distributed gloves and sweetmeats among the invited. To conclude the ceremony, the President had the doctor seated at his side, while he extended greetings and benedictions.

7

WHAT IS A DOCTOR?—PARACELSUS—THE GLORY OF SACRIFICE—ABSOLUTION—FLAVIUS JOSEPHUS—FATHER-MOTHER

"*Abios, Bios Bios Abiatos*" (Without health life is not life). Such was the motto of Doctor François Rabelais, who considered it his solemn duty to try to bring health, and therefore life, to all who sought his ministrations. And he possessed the necessary personal magnetism, as attested by many of his contemporaries.

"There must be nothing about the physician, even to his fingernails, which may give offense to the patient. On the other hand, everything about the doctor, his face, his gestures, his clothing, his conversation, the glance of his eye, his touch, must be calculated to please and soothe the sick one. And that is what I am engaged in doing to the best of my abilities. A peevish, grouchy, crabby, unpleasant and ill-humored face on the part of the physician tends to give his patients the blues, whereas a jovial, serene, pleasant, smiling, and open countenance cheers the patient."

Rabelais' theory of curing was a balance of mind and body and their reciprocity of preserving and restoring health, the mind taking the initiative, with emphasis on the value of enjoyment, cheerfulness, merriment, humor,

pleasure and high spirits. Science, therefore, working
with Nature, with *Physis* as *against* Nature—*Anti-Physis*.

The Humanist physician, despite his vow to Hippocrates, substituted for the authority of the Latins that
of the Arabs and particularly of the Jewish doctors,
who were noted for independent thinking and their ad-
diction to empiricism.

And there was Paracelsus (1493-1541) who disdained
them all. His real name was Theophrastus Bombast von
Hohenheim. His father was a physician and his mother
superintendent of the hospital of Einsildeln. He adopted
the epithet of Paracelsus to denote both his admiration
and his superiority over Celsus.

Celsus was a second-century physician and opponent
of Christianity. Agnostic and skeptic, Celsus said: "Jesus
was born in adultery and nurtured on the wisdom of
Egypt. His assertion of divine dignity is disproved by
his poverty and his miserable end. The idea of an Incar-
nation of God is absurd. Why should the human race
think itself so superior to bees, ants and elephants as
to be put in this unique relation to its maker? And why
should God choose to come to men as a Jew? The
Christian idea of special providence is nonsense, an insult
to the deity. Christians are like a council of frogs in a
marsh or a synod of worms on a dunghill, croaking and
squeaking: 'For our sakes was the world created.' It
is much more reasonable to believe that each part of
the world has its own special deity; prophets and super-
natural messengers have forsooth appeared in more
places than one. Besides being bad philosophy based on
fictitious history, Christianity is not respectable. The
qualifications for conversion are ignorance and childish
timidity. Like all quacks they gather a crowd of slaves,
children, women and idlers. The rogue, the thief, the
burglar, the poisoner, the spoiler of temples and tombs

are their proselytes. They pretend that God will save the unjust man if he repents and humbles himself. The just man who has held steady from the cradle in the ways of virtue Jesus will not look upon."

Paracelsus attached no value to mere scholarship. He, therefore, went wandering all over Europe to learn all he could at first hand, and was one of the first physicians of modern times to profit by a mode of study which is now considered indispensable. "The book of Nature is that which the physician must read, and to do so he must walk over the leaves. Every faculty of medicine is a nest of fools, rogues and assassins, and the worst of them all are the medical-priest crew, who not only poison and maim their victims but add prayers to their bill. Follow me, Avicenna, Galen, Rhasia, Motagna, Mesus! Follow me from Paris, from Montpellier, from Cologne, from Vienna! Greek, Arab, Israelite, follow me, not I you! Of you no one will survive, even in the most distant corner! I shall be the Monarch; mine will be the Monarchy!"

On November 1, 1532, François Rabelais was appointed sole physician to the famous "Grand Hostel-Dieu de Notre Dame de Pitié du Pont-du-Rhône," in Lyons. His salary was 40 livres a year, the same as that of the "barber-surgeon," who accompanied him on his rounds and followed his instructions, since being a man of the Church, he was not allowed to operate.

The hospital was a large hall, divided by pillars and a lattice, six rows of beds with walnut bedsteads and tapestry hangings, all clean, white and well-fitted out, so that the patients could see the chapel at the end of the hall, where Mass was said daily. On one side were the men, on the other the women, and in the center a large fireplace where they warmed themselves in the winter. There was also a maternity annex and one for contagious cases. The patients numbered between 150 and 220, sleeping two or three in one large bed. There were sixteen nurses, white-robed Magdalens, numerous servants, a resident apothecary, a "barber-surgeon" and a curate.

The physician had to pay a daily visit, and Rabelais was so successful that the mortality among the patients dropped soon after his appointment. Modern medical men credit him with competence in connection with syphilis and mercurial stomatitis from inunctions, and familiarity with the uterine origin of hysteria. He had proficiency in surgical anatomy and invented two surgical instruments, one for the reduction of fractures of the thighbone and the other for operating in cases of strangulated hernia.

Rabelais' knowledge, though somewhat confused, shows an advance beyond the Galenic doctrine of two kinds of blood, prevalent in his day, but it stops short of that of his younger contemporary, Miguel Servetus (1511-1553), Spanish physician and scholar, believed by some to be the discoverer of the circulation of blood, burned by Calvin because of his advanced theological opinions, in particular the negation of the Trinity—*De Trinitatis Erroribus* (1531).

On the psychological side, Rabelais derided the anagogic dream interpretation and emphasized the value of laughter as an emotional release. He also won distinction as botanist and was in advance of all writers of his day in the nomenclature and the origin of names of plants, and the first one to have any idea of the existence of sex among them.

While at the Hostel-Dieu, Rabelais made dissections, which, although practiced in Italy for two centuries, was a novelty for France, the Faculty of Medicine of Paris being entitled to the body of one criminal a year. Moreover, these dissections were performed in a perfunctory and ignorant manner by the "barber-surgeon," who acted as prosector to the professor, the latter rarely handling the knife, and in general being less competent than the barber.

Vesalius, who attended lectures in Paris between 1533 and 1536, records the difficulties surrounding a student of human anatomy in this early dawn of science. He himself used to prowl around the gibbet at Montfaucon and fight with the dogs for the arm or leg of the criminal.

Andreas Vesalius (1514-1564), Flemish physician, was the founder of the modern system of anatomy. He was professor of anatomy at Pavia, Bologna and Pisa, and became chief physician to Emperor Charles V. His *De Humani Corporis Fabrica* (1543) was considered "an immortal work, by which all that had been written before was almost superseded."

The Holy Inquisition condemned Vesalius to death for heresy, but commuted the sentence to a pilgrimage to the Holy Sepulchre. It is not recorded whether his visit to the Holyland changed his mind. At any rate, he learned that sanity in a mad world was disastrous, and wisdom counseled mimicry of the symptoms of the disease for mutual reassurance.

Once Rabelais dissected publicly a man who had been hanged. Etienne Dolet, who had already made a name for himself among Humanists, unaware that before too many years would pass he himself would suffer the fate of the executed man, celebrated Rabelais' deed in Latin verse, making the victim speak: "Strangled by the fatal knot, I was hanging miserably on the gallows. Unexpected good fortune which I had scarcely dared ask of the Great Jupiter! The eyes of a vast assembly are centered upon me; I am dissected by the most learned of doctors, who will hold for admiration in the machinery of my body, the incomparable order, the sublime beauty of the structure of the human anatomy, masterpiece of the Creator. The crowd is looking on all attention. What a signal honor and what excess of glory! And to think that I might have been the plaything of the winds, the prey of wheeling and rapacious crows! Ah! Fate may now do its worst against me. I am transported with glory!"

It was neither irony nor gallows humor, but a Humanistic attitude toward man in his relation to man, and proof of his eventual perfectability.

During the next few years Rabelais' ecclesiastical position became more and more untenable. However, with the elevation to the Pontificate of Paul III (1468-1549), who showed strong sympathy for the Reform movement within the Church, he thought it opportune to straighten himself out. He deposited in the Papal Chancery a supplication *pro apostasia*. In it he confessed that he had abandoned the religious life, that he had changed the habit of monk for that of a secular priest, had traveled about the world, studied medicine in which he had taken three degrees, and practiced it, celebrating occasionally Mass and taking part in other services of the Church. He expressed great contrition and begged the Holy Father to grant him absolution from the taint of apostasy, and to be empowered to practice the art of medicine within the canonical limits, that is, up to the application of the knife and the fire exclusively, and for purely humanitarian reasons, without the expectation of lucre or gain.

His request was granted in a letter by the Pontiff, dated January 17, 1536. "Wishing to succor with gracious favor one who has received manifold commendations for zeal of religion, knowledge of letters, honesty of life and morals, and other merits of probity and virtue, and having these things in view, we do hereby absolve you." And the Holy Father further granted his "beloved son" all that he asked for.

It should not have been an ordeal of conscience for the Pope to forgive the vagaries of Doctor François Rabelais, for he was "the last of the Renaissance Pontiffs," more Humanist than Christian. He believed that Christianity consisted of a grain of fact and a ton of fiction, and that to deal with the world one had to employ a grain of truth and a ton of hypocrisy, since it was in these proportions that mankind could digest facts and truth. Moreover, he was always aware that politically he was the Pontifex Maximus, the Roman Emperor, and acted accordingly.

Nor would it have been difficult for Paul to understand and dismiss sins of Venus, since he could not very well cast stones around, living as he did, in a glass house. "You ask," Rabelais writes in a letter to a friend, while he was in Rome, "if Pierluigi is the legitimate son or bastard of Pope Paul III. I would inform you that the Pope was never married, which is equivalent to stating that the aforementioned is literally a bastard. At this time the Pope is keeping a Roman lady of the Casa Ruffina, by whom he had a daughter, who married Lord Bosso, Count of Santa Fiore, and also one of the Little Cardinals, who is known as the Cardinal of Santa Fiore."

But Rabelais does not mean to belittle the Pontiff. On the contrary, he has the highest regard for his scholarship and his patronage of artists. Alexander Farnese, who became Pope Paul III, on October 1, 1534, was a member of an old and distinguished family. He loved beauty and magnificence in various forms, and on September 1, 1535, appointed Michelangelo chief architect, painter and sculptor to the Vatican, commissioning him to paint "The Last Judgment."

And Rabelais adds that "Paul is poorer than any Pope of the last three hundred years," which is proof patent that he was an honest man, and in this respect, at least, he obeyed the precept of his Lord.

Georges d'Armagnac, Bishop of Rhodez, friend of letters and of François Rabelais, commissioned him to deliver to Erasmus a copy of the works of Flavius Josephus (37-95), the Jewish historian and military commander.

Josephus belonged to one of the holiest priestly families of Palestine. After studying the various sects of Judaism—Pharisee, Sadducee and Essene—he became a member of the Pharisees, which may be interpreted as "Separatists," indicating their devotion to the ideal of a nation separate from all others by virtue of its peculiar relation to Yahweh. However, they were eager to make converts and some of their greatest teachers were of non-Jewish parentage. They insisted upon the strict observance of the Law, as far as it was compatible with ordinary life, and the disciples were to set a proper example to the masses.

Josephus had been to Rome and had obtained an introduction to Empress Poppae. He could witness the great imperial power, and upon his return to Jerusalem he tried to convince the Jews not to revolt against Rome. He was not listened to and was dragged into the Great Rebellion of the year 66.

In the spring of 67, the Jewish troops, whom Josephus had so sedulously trained, fled before the Roman forces of Vespasian and Titus. With the stragglers, who remained, Josephus held a stronghold against the Romans by dint of his native cunning. Finally, when the place was taken, he persuaded the forty men who shared his hiding place to kill one another rather than commit suicide or surrender. They agreed to cast lots, on the understanding that the second one should kill the first one, and so on.

Fortunately Josephus drew the last lot and persuaded his destined victim to live. Whether he agreed is not known, but Josephus survived, surrendered, and was led before Vespasian. He was inspired to prophecy (by what sign is not recorded) that he would become emperor.

In consequence of this he was spared but kept in prison until the prophecy should come to pass, which it did two years later. When freed, Josephus assumed the name of Flavius, the family name of Vespasian, and accompanied his patron to Alexandria.

He returned to attend Titus and act as intermediary between him and the Jews, when the city fell in the year 70. Now Titus granted him whatever boon he desired, and Josephus secured the lives of a few men who had saved the Sacred Books. He repaired to Rome, where he was made a Roman citizen and received an estate in Judaea. Thereafter, he devoted his life to literary work under the patronage of Vespasian, Titus and Domitian.

Josephus wrote *The Jewish War,* and while the original Aramaic manuscript has been lost, the Greek version, which he himself prepared, survived. In it he praises the valor of the Jewish soldier, but also does honor to the Romans. His *Jewish Antiquities* covers in twenty books the history of the Jews from the creation of the world to the outbreak of the Roman War. Its purpose was to glorify the Jews in the Roman eyes.

The accounts of John the Baptist and of Jesus are interpolations, and it is quite evident that Josephus knew nothing of Jesus, proof either of his nonexistence or nonimportance at the time, since little escaped the keen eye and the prolific pen of the great historian.

Desiderius Erasmus (1467-1536) was in Basle. How lovely Basle used to be—a neat little city, streets clean, citizens dignified and courteous, paying allegiance neither to war-mongering princes nor to war-mongering monks. And how it had changed! Rome and Basle—two centers of fanaticism, Protestant and Catholic. And before long Erasmus would be in grave danger from both sides, and only a native shrewdness protected him—that and death.

For the moment, however, he was still the intellectual lighthouse of Europe—*"Doctor Universalis,"* "Prince of Scientific Learning," "Father of Study," "Light of the World."

"Everyone who does not wish to remain a stranger in the realm of the Muses admires him, glorifies him, sings his praises."

And François Rabelais, as he sent him the books of Josephus, added a letter of gratitude to the man who cracked the night of superstition and afforded him personally the joy of knowledge and understanding, disdain for scholasticism and dogmatism and hatred for religious fanaticism.

"I have eagerly seized the opportunity, O Humanest of Fathers, to prove to you by grateful homage my profound respect for you and my filial piety. My Father, did I say? I should call you Mother, did your indulgence allow it. For the truth is, that those who carry a child in their womb guard an absolutely unknown offspring, whose face they have never seen, from the dangers of the surrounding world; and what have you shown toward me, but this very affection? You have educated me, though unknown to your face and in name. You have suckled me from the most chaste breasts of your celestial learning. So that if I do not put down to you all that I am and all that I am worth, it should be the standing example of monstrous ingratitude now and forever. So I salute you again and again, most dear

Father, glory of your country, defender of the freedom of letters, unconquerable champion of truth. Goodbye and all good luck remain with you. Lyons, December 1532. Yours, as much as his own, Franciscus Rabelaesus, Medicus."

It is unfortunate that the reply of Erasmus is lost, for certainly there was one, since the great Dutchman, friend of kings and princes, and of universal peace among all men, was the epitome of courtesy and gentleness.

Political conditions during the first thirty-seven years of the sixteenth century were turbulent, what with the wars of Charles V, who in 1530 was crowned by Pope Clement VII as King of Lombardy and Emperor of the Romans, the last coronation of a German Emperor by a Pope, sacking and burning the Eternal City, and the perennial dynastic skirmishes in all parts of the continent.

Yet the Humanistic pot was boiling and people drank of the heady brew, and Rabelais dared to write: "The masters of the Sorbonne made a vow never to take a bath or wipe their noses until there should be a definite ruling in the matter. For which reason, they are to this day both dirty and snotty."

And Etienne Dolet (prosecuted as murderer of the painter Guillaume Compaign, but in self-defense, and pardoned by the King) could give a banquet at which the guests dared to talk about the finest foreign writers: Erasmus, Melanchton, Bembo, Sadolet, Vida, More, Sannazar, and greet each name with loud acclamation.

In a Latin poem commemorating the event, Etienne Dolet enumerates his guests: "There were those whom we justly call the luminaries of France: Budé, the first in every branch of learning; Berauld, fortunate in his natural endowments and his flowing eloquence; Danès, distinguished in all arts; Toussaint, deservedly called 'the living library'; Macrin, to whom Apollo has given empire over every kind of poetry; Bourbon, likewise rich in poetic treasure; Dampierre; Voulté, who inspires the learned world with high hopes; Marot, that Gallic Virgil, who shows a divine force in his poetry; and finally François Rabelais, the honor and glory of the healing art, who even from the threshold of Pluto can recall the dead and restore them to the light."

All these writers, whether writing in the vernacular or in Latin, were Humanists, fighting against obscurantism and the Sorbonne. There was a definite tie between them and the Protestants, although later they realized that Calvinism had little in common with their dream of the free life, and his predestination thundered from Geneva alienated them completely. To the Humanists religion meant a return to something like primitive Christianity, unencumbered by traditional forms and ritualistic observances.

On the other hand, Calvin said: "François Rabelais, after having tasted of the Gospel, has been struck with blindness. He and the other mad dogs who vomit their ordure in the very presence of the Majesty of God, have endeavored to pervert all religion."

8

EDITOR—REVISER—TRANSLATOR—
PYGMIES AND GIANTS

*L*yons was the center of the primary industry and the home of a brilliant group of men of letters, scholars and Humanists. Untainted by the blighting influence of the Sorbonne, and situated at the crossroads of Europe, where Italy, France, Germany and Switzerland met and passed, it became the most cosmopolitan city of the West and the money market for foreign exchange. Merchants of all countries flocked to Rue Mercière.

And to Rue Mercière came Sebastian Gryphius, Latin scholar from Württemberg, Swabia, in the year 1524, and founded the publishing house "At the Sign of the Griffin," which was to become one of the most famous of France. Besides pocket editions of the classics, Gryphius published Greek and Latin texts celebrated for their beauty.

To Lyons there also came in the summer of 1532 Maître François Rabelais, Medicus, in search of a job which would be more gainful than the practice of his profession, and he found it "At the Sign of the Griffin."

On June 3, 1532, there appeared a volume of Latin letters on medicine by Giovanni Manardi of Ferrara— *Epistolae Medicinales Manardi,* edited by François Rabelais and dedicated to his friend and adviser, jurist André Tiraqueau (1480-1558), author of *De Legibus Connubialibus* (The Laws of Marriage), published in

1513 and 1515, a volume of six hundred pages, which had a great success.

The book was considered an attack on woman; as a matter of fact, however, it is a juridical attempt at fair-mindedness, presenting evidence on both sides of the problem, as far as it is compatible with the author's doctrine (and universally accepted) that woman is by nature inferior to man, and that therefore she must obey and man command.

Tiraqueau himself was very happy in his own marriage, which meant that he graciously allowed himself to be henpecked. From such a secure vantage point he dared speak of the inferiority of woman, his wife nodding and smiling cunningly, taking revenge on her female friends who were devoured with envy and jealousy. The evil that man speaks of woman is streaked with love; the good that woman speaks of woman is dipped in the vinegar of contempt.

Tiraqueau advised his fellow men in matters of matrimony. "Take a mate who is neither too good-looking nor yet too homely. The same station in life is the better rule, though marrying into the nobility is not to be excluded. Avoid widows and old maids. Marry at thirty-six a woman of eighteen. Make inquiries concerning your prospective wife's family, nationality and character.

"The education of a wife must include the fact that she should not consider herself her husband's equal. She is not to be struck or mistreated in any way. She is to be educated by example and by caresses mingled with severity. The husband is to be careful not to reveal his personal secrets to her. What a woman does not tell when awake, she will not fail to tell in her sleep. Marital fidelity is obligatory for both husband and wife, and the antidote for adultery is poison. Yet, if in spite of all precautions, your wife turns out to be immodest, remember to bear it patiently."

And Madame Tiraqueau bent over her distaff and dreamed little dreams.

While in the first editions of *The Laws of Marriage* Tiraqueau wrote eulogistic passages about Rabelais, in the third, since Rabelais was under a cloud due to the censorship of the Sorbonne, he elided them, and later he was one of the judges condemning his work.

At this same period François Rabelais edited and published the *Aphorisms of Hippocrates* together with the *Ars Parva of* Galen, books on which he had lectured at Montpellier, and added a commentary in both Latin and Greek and an epistle to his patron, Bishop Geoffroy d'Estissac, also two Latin legal documents, a will and a contract of sales, "relics of venerable antiquity."

He dedicated this on September 4, 1532, to his friend Aymery Bouchard. Always generous, since he had nothing to give, Rabelais offered his books. And in his last will and testament he said: "I possess nothing; the rest I give to the poor." He lined tragedies with humor, and hid in vulgarities noble truths.

The *"Relics"* turned out to be forgeries by an Italian Humanist. This, however, was not discovered until thirty years after Rabelais' death. It is quite possible, however, that Rabelais had suspected the treachery, but practical joker that he was, pretended ignorance. He filled his own books with burlesque learning, deliberately making mistakes. He would roar with laughter if he saw the variorum edition of his works wherein scholars solemnly have corrected his errors, their footnotes bulking much larger than the text.

Because these books did not indemnify the publisher for the cost of printing or perhaps because they did not yield the high profit he had anticipated, Gryphius grumbled: *"Ach! die Franzosen!"* Rabelais, always the optimist, made a solemn vow: "By Jupiter, I will repair your losses, Meister Gryphius! Moreover, I swear by Him,

God of all the gods, that the name of Franciscus Rabelaesus, Medicus, now only known to a few, will soon be
in the mouths of all and in the hands of all, so that his
fame will be as great abroad as at home!"

And Jupiter hearkened unto the vow of one whom
He considered an adopted son of Greece, and granted
his prayer a hundredfold, nay, a thousandfold. Even the
book of *Aphorisms* and *Ars Parva,* which at first had
disappointed the publisher, proved to be a "sleeper,"
and eventually sold enough to warrant a second edition
in 1543.

While Rabelais was doing works of erudition for Sebastian Gryphius, which gave him a place of honor
among men of letters and science, he also contracted
with Claude Nourry, a printer and publisher of popular
vernacular literature, the editing of almanacs. "Almanac
Calculated upon the Meridian of the worthy City of
Lyons and the Climate of the Kingdom, Composed by
me, François Rabelais, Doctor of Medicine and Professor of Astrology, etc."

It was tongue-in-cheek, yet the almanacs proved in-
valuable in the later judgment of Rabelais' mind and
attitudes. He threaded the pleasantries and vulgar jests
with maxims of profound wisdom and criticisms, which
he would not have dared to do in his scholarly treatises,
for he knew that the Sorbonne would not deign to
glance at the material dished out to the *profanum
vulgus.*

The almanacs offered, as was customary, not only
the dominical letters and other similar information, but
prophecies of coming events, based on astrological science. As if to remove all blame from himself, the shrewd
monk says: "So far as I can see, astrological prognostica-
tions are looked down upon by all men of learning, who
call it a cheat and a vanity, because of the silliness of
those who have dealt with the subject, and because of

the failure each year of promises so made to come true. I shall, therefore, refrain for the time being from telling you what I have found in the calculations of Cl. Ptolomaeus."

And now he turns clown, which he knew would please the ignorant, who at all times, and everywhere, distrust the men of intellect, often enough for good reason, since many of them use it to enslave those who lack it. "But I shall tell you that this year crabs will go sideways and ropemakers backwards; stools will climb on benches, spits on the andirons, and hats on the heads. Fleas will be black for the most part. As for dice, they won't say what you want them to, and luck won't always come your way. The blind this year will see very little and the deaf will have trouble enough trying to hear, while the dumb will not have a great deal to say. Old age will be incurable this year, on account of the years past."

And to flatter the commoner, but at the same time to slap most thunderously the brazen cheek of the professional astrologer, Rabelais adds: "At any rate, the greatest folly in the world is to think that there are stars for kings, popes and great lords rather than for the poor and the suffering; as if new stars had been created since the time of the Flood, or since Romulus or Pharamond, and the new kings."

Yet to make certain that if some bigot of the hierarchy inadvertently came across his almanac there would be no cause for gathering faggots, Rabelais further disclaims all knowledge of the future, while proclaiming all reverence for the Creator. "These are secrets of the close counsel of the Eternal King, who rules, according to His free will and good pleasure, everything that is and that is done."

It took courage to decry astrology even behind the transparent fog of impersonality, for there existed at the time a widespread belief in it, even among men of intellectual eminence. There was, for instance, Michel de Notredame, of Jewish origin, who called himself Nostradamus.

Nostradamus (1503-1566) was born at St. Remi in Provence on the 13th of December, 1503. After studying the humanities at Avignon, he took the degree of Doctor of Medicine at Montpellier in 1529. At Aix and at Lyons he acquired great distinction by his labors during outbreaks of the plague. In 1555 he published in Lyons a book of rhymed prophecies, under the title of *Centuries,* which secured him the notice of Catherine de' Medici; and in 1558 he published an enlarged edition with a dedication to the King. The seeming fulfilment of some of his predictions increased his influence, and Charles IX named him physician in ordinary. He died on July 2, 1566.

The *Centuries* of Nostradamus have been frequently reprinted, and in 1781 were condemned by the papal court, being supposed to contain a prediction of the fall of the papacy. It may yet be that his only error was the timing thereof. And what are centuries to the divinities but a winking of their eyes, and all things march toward their end.

Paracelsus alone, of all the scientific contemporaries of Rabelais rejected astrology.

Several editions of the almanac were published during the life of Rabelais, the date being altered to suit the year, until 1542, when *L'an Perpetuel* (Perpetual Year) was substituted for the date of the particular year, and the last of the series appeared in 1550.

Man seems unable to crawl out of the variegated fog of his infancy and ever clamors for tales of giants and ogres, wizards and witches, gods and demons, saints and villains, fairies and hobgoblins—all recalling the dim days when he was a helpless dwarf among those gigantic creatures who were his father and mother and aunts and uncles and neighbors, tending him, teaching him, punishing him, and doing strange and marvelous deeds, which made him shiver and laugh and weep and love and hate.

The Arthurian Cycle gave birth to many folk-tales of this sort, the most spectacular being the one of Gargantua and his family. By art-magic the celebrated Enchanter Merlin of the Round Table created two enormous giants to defend King Arthur, Grangousier and Gargamelle, his wife, together with a great mare to carry them. From their mating was born the giant Gargantua. Catching a fever in Brittany, the parent-giants died of a purgative and young Gargantua went to Paris. After astonishing the citizens with many wondrous feats, he returned to Brittany, whence Merlin conveyed him on a cloud to England. Here with his great club he helped King Arthur rout Gog and Magog and the Dutch and Irish hordes, taking prisoner their king and fifty of the nobility and packing them all into a hollow tooth that had bothered him, in lieu of a dental filling. Having performed many other extraordinary feats and having served Arthur for two hundred years, three months and four days, he was transported to Fairyland by Morgan Le Fay and Mélusine. And thus the story ends.

Throughout Europe during the Middle Ages and earlier still there sprouted countless legends of giant heroes who were in the habit of residing or passing through a certain place, and who were noted for their prowess, their enormous size, their appetites. Each of these personages possessed an individual name and a history. In time, however, they were all absorbed into the one monolithic giant—Gargantua.

Scattered over France there are rocks, stones, dolmens and menhirs, megalithic monuments bearing names connected with the Giant: Gargantua's finger; Gargantua's tooth; Gargantua's spoon; Gargantua's chair; Gargantua's cane; Gargantua's shoes; Gargantua's *pierre à pisser;* Gargantua's tomb.

Like a princess, a legend may be asleep for a long period, but someday some "prince" will arrive to awaken it. The Gargantuan tale, half-buried in the ruins of literature was "awakened" suddenly by the learned Doctor François Rabelais, who revised it for the printer, Claude Nourry. It was in the form of a small quarto volume of sixty-four leaves without the name of the printer, editor, or precise date of publication.

"Les grandes et inestimables Chronicques du grand et énorme géant Gargantua; Contenant sa géneolgie, la Grandeur et force de son corps. Aussi le merueil des faicts darmes quil fist pour le Roy Artus, comme verrez ci aprez. Imprime nouuelement, 1532."

(The Great and Inestimable Chronicle of the Great and Enormous Giant Gargantua: Containing his Geneology, the Size and Strength of His Body. Also the Marvelous Feats of Arms which he Performed for King Arthur, as will be hereinafter Revealed. Newly Printed, 1532.)

As was customary, the book made its appearance at the August Lyons fair. There were four fairs during the year, and they became internationally famous—a wonderland of merchandise with hucksters coming from all countries. The book trade flourished at these fairs, and generally speaking, publishers brought out their wares only at these seasons.

Evidently Rabelais' book came on time, for time is the measure of success. "It sold more copies in two months than Bibles had sold in nine years."

How much money Rabelais derived from his labors is unknown, but literary returns in those days were generally almost nil. An author was fortunate if, when the book came out, the publisher, who was also the printer and the bookseller, had the courtesy to write him a little note of thanks and to include a *"douceur"*—a little something to soothe his nerves and fill his belly. But François Rabelais would soon be appointed as physician at "Hostel-Dieu," and what with the stipend and the "little purses" his patrons and friends would mail him in reply to his urgent pleas, he managed to keep body and soul together. If the soul was pleased with this union or was irked by it cannot be determined, for not even the most learned theologian can say with precision whether the soul is a delighted guest or an impatient prisoner seeking escape from the foul tomb of guts in which man imprisons it, life being predicated on their perpetual refilling.

9

EVE'S BASTARD AND HIS WAYS— PANTAGRUEL, ROY DES DIPSODES— RIDENDO DICERE VERUM— BETWEEN TWO WORLDS

*I*t was the summer of 1532, and never in the memory of man had there been such a drought.

Was Lord Yahweh up to His old tricks again? Since He could not get rid of man by Flood, would He try it now by removing the waters?

Daily were the processions throughout the land, praying for rain. "Let Thy great mouth, O Lord, be a vast spout, pouring water upon us! The flames of Hell are piercing through the Earth devouring our fields and our cattle, and our parched gullets spit cotton.

"We deserve our punishment—*Tu autem, Domine, miserere nobis*—but O Lord, have mercy upon us! We have broken all Thy commandments again and again, and many and vile are our sins! We cheat one another. We rob one another. We hate one another. We slay one another. And Thy priests, the shepherds of the flocks, are worse than wolves. Yea, we are savage sinners, yet have mercy upon us, O Lord! Do not destroy us utterly!

"Tear open the clouds! Let their waters pour upon us, O Lord! *Te Deum laudamus! In nomine Patris et Filii et Spiritus Sancti, Amen!*"

As the buzzing of importunate flies were the clam-

73

orous lamentations about the ears of Yahweh walking in His garden, millions of light-years distant from the Earth, which He in His infinite folly and to His infinite regret had created.

"He still annoys Me, Eve's bastard!" Yahweh muttered. "And as always he asks for undeserved favors. He has split Me into three, and made of Me a monster. Once, while still in Eden, I created a three-headed sheep. It was thrice as stupid as the rest of the flock and the bleating that issued from its three gullets sickened Me. I turned it into a stone and set it at the gate, as a warning to man never to create monstrosities. Yet he created Me in the image of the three-headed sheep, and now has the brazenness to implore my aid in his survival.

"Whoever it is attempting to clear the earth of its vicious despoiler, he will not succeed, since I, craftier than all the Gods and all the Devils put together, could not accomplish it.

"Yet in due time the arrogant braggart will pluck the ultimate kernel I placed for his safety at the core of life, and thus he will perish by his own hand.

"As for now, let him burn! I will not succor him by emptying my bladder upon his ugly head! Ah, why did I create him in My own image? In truth, however, he created *Me* in *his* own image—jealous, pretentious, vainglorious, vindictive, bellicose, cruel. And when he *did* create Me gentle and peace-loving, He crucified Me and made Me a scapegoat. With *My* blood he would cleanse himself, the wily hypocrite!

"Ah, let Me forget! Let Me forget!" He waved the terrestrial buzzing from His ears and quaffed out of a hollowed star the wine He squeezed from the Grape of the Moon, which dispels all thoughts and grants the bliss of ignorance.

"In order to understand fully the cause and reason

of the name of Pantagruel, which was given him in baptism, you should note that there was that year so great a drought throughout the land of Africa that thirty-six months, three weeks, four days and a little more than thirteen hours passed without rain, and with the sun so hot that the whole earth was dried up. There was not a single tree on earth that had either leaf or flower. The grass was without any green, the riverbeds were empty; the fountains dry; the poor fish, tired of their own element, wandered over the earth, crying horribly; the birds fell from the air for lack of dew; and the wolves, the foxes, the deer, the wild boars, the hares, the rabbits, the weasels, the martens, the badgers, and all other beasts were to be found dead in the fields, their jaws drooping open. As to human beings, that was a pity indeed. You might have seen them with their tongues hanging out like rabbits that had been running for six hours; some cast themselves into the bottom of wells, while others crawled into the bellies of cows to find shade. On Friday, when everybody was begging the Almighty in procession for rain, drops began falling, and as they began to try to catch a little of this dew, they found that it was nothing but brine, saltier and worse-tasting than sea water. And inasmuch as it was this very day that Pantagruel was born, his father named him as he did; for *panta* in Greek is equivalent to *all* and *gruel* in the Hagarene language is equivalent to *thirsty,* the inference being that at the child's birth the world was *all athirst*—and therefore, *pantagruel, Roy des Dipsodes*—King of the Thirsty Ones."

Pantagruel was a *petit diable* or *diablotin,* a minor character in the mystery plays dating from the fifteenth century and continuing into the sixteenth century, as well as the name of a malady affecting the throat.

Pantagruel's business was to watch over the "sea

wastes," and therefore was all covered with salt. During his leisure moments, he amused himself by stealthily casting salt down the throats of drunkards, "and he did it better than a pair of hoary devils." Oh, how the audience roared with laughter, for what is funnier than a dipsomaniac hugging his bottle and staggering across the stage hiccoughing?

The French theater of the time was distinctly popular. Actors and audiences indiscriminately mingled. The witticisms and the gags were as familiar to the spectators as to the actors, and they were earthy and vulgar, yet innocent withal, for their purpose was not to excite, but rather to quench passion by mockery and laughter—burlesques without pretentions.

The Great and Inestimable Chronicle of the Great and Enormous Giant Gargantua, which Rabelais edited, was a hodge-podge of stories without logical sequence or literary structure, but as he read them to his patients they laughed, and laughter, according to him, was the basic drug in the pharmacopoeia of Nature.

One day, as he took his usual walk through the noisy and manure-filled streets of Lyons, an idea struck the Medicus. Under similar circumstances Socrates would have been certain that it was his good daemon whispering into his ear. If this preposterous Giant and his silly deeds amuse the poor souls, why don't I write something more genial and more efficacious for their recovery? Take that little rascal Pantagruel, for instance, does he have to pour salt into the throats of drunkards forever? Can't I make him do more interesting deeds? Can't I endow him with a sting in his tongue and a hook to his foot to annoy the bigots and the pretentious? What would be half as funny as watching them squirm, when the little devil mocked them or kicked their posteriors? I must take great care, of course, never "to get too near the fire." No idea, however brilliant, deserves one's toasted skin. But under a laugh one can hide a worm burrowing its way into a solemn rectum.

"*Ridendo dicere verum,*" as Lucian said—Lucian, that great laugher of ancient days, that spurner of the gods, those upon Olympus, those in the clouds, and those who spread their fat arses upon earth. How well he knew that men's actions and conduct fell far short of their professions, and that their professions themselves were generally worthless and a mere guise to secure popularity and reward. And as for the philosophers—what did he say about them? If I ever meet one on the road I will shun him, as I would a mad dog. But Lucian was fortunate to live in safer days, when there was no Sorbonne and its black doctors. He could not have shunned *them.* They would have jumped at his throat, if his nose had dared to even crease at their sight.

What more did Lucian say? Without regard for men and gods seek thou sound reason as remedy for vanity and superstition, and tell the truth laughing—*Ridendo dicere verum!* That shall be my motto as well!

Doctor François Rabelais went to his lodging, seated himself at the table, dipped his goose quill into the enormous inkstand, and began to write in his beautiful hand. He wrote on and on, hour after hour. Now he would guffaw; now he would smile; and once in a while his sharp eyes would gaze in amazement at what he had put on the paper. He was certain he had not meant to do it, that the words had somehow written themselves and would not be uprooted, his pen refusing to draw lines across them. They belonged there by some right he could not dispute.

What was the meaning of this? Was art a diver recovering from the bed of the Sea of Forgetfulness bits of the cargoes shipwrecked in the gale of time? Had they been his own experiences in days long passed, their memories hibernating somewhere in the back of his brain, awakening at propitious moments? Or were they, perchance, the experiences of his ancestors, transmitted with their blood into his veins?

Never did one escape one's ancestors, of that he was certain, and the gifts they bequeathed had to be carefully scrutinized, many of them being Trojan horses filled with prejudices and superstitions. *Et dona ferentes*—beware of the gifts of the Greeks—and many an ancestor turned Greek.

On a few occasions during the dissections at Montpellier, he opened craniums and tried to read what was recorded in the tortuous valleys of the brain, but he discovered no caverns, no secret gates leading to false cemeteries. Did people really die, or was burial but a farce? And the soul, where did it lodge? At what moment did it enter the fetus? How long did it have to wait to take its turn in the infinite caravan of souls? Did it have the right of choice or was its host predestined? By what aperture did it leave the body—the nostrils, the ears, the mouth, the anus? Did it leave it with the last breath of the moribund, or, anticipating the end and fearful that it might remain in the corpse and share in its corruption and dissolution, did it fly out before, in the manner of rats dashing out of sinking ships? And did it ever happen that the host recovered and the soul could not re-enter it, and wandered about disconsolate until the host died? Were they discriminated against by veritable ghosts?

The theologians had pat answers for everything, and brooked no questions, detecting in them seeds of doubt, mistrust and antagonism, and it was perilous to ask them. They dealt in words, and words had the habit of devouring the ideas which had given them birth, and ended by meaning nothing, and in their hollowness tyrannized over the minds of men.

As for himself, he was interested only in facts discovered by using one's hands and one's eyes and one's
free mind, unafraid of the truth, whatever it might be,
wherever it might lead, even if it blew as a hurricane
toppling one's most cherished notions. But always watch
out—*caveat semper!* This device he would carve on his
coat-of-arms!

If only he were allowed to use the scalpel and the
lancet himself, not be forced to entrust them into the
clumsy hands of the barber, ripping and tearing. He
was a priest and therefore might not cut into living flesh,
nor even into the dead. How then could he delve into
the recesses of the delicate organs? The Jews ordered
their priests not to shed blood, and millennia later, the
representatives of Christ must obey their injunction, at
the same time hounding and degrading and murdering
their descendants, for there was no command against
roasting and garroting. Ah, let us drink! Ah, let us
laugh!

Maître Rabelais wrote on and on, borrowing on all
sides, for great inventors are great borrowers, and origi-
nality is but the turning of dull clay into glowing marble.
And he "builded better than he knew," for that is the
way of the artist. He may not know the root that feeds
the flower. He who ventures to expose the root and
examine it, kills the flower. He is the critic.

Sometime during the month of September, Rabelais
brought his manuscript to his publisher, who set it in
the usual format of a small quarto of 64 leaves under the
title: *Les horribles et espouvantables Faictz et Prouesses
du tresnomme Pantagruel, Roy des Dipsodes, Filz du
grant Geant Gargantua: composez nouvellement par
Maistre Alcofribas Nasier, Abstracteur de Quintessence.*
(The Horrible and Terrible Deeds and Prowesses of
the Much Renowned Pantagruel, King of Dipsodes, Son

of the Great Giant Gargantua: Recently Composed by Master Alcofribas Nasier, Abstracter of the Fifth Essence.)

And so without a date and concealing the author's name under an anagram, the book appeared at the Lyons November fair.

The following year, François Juste, his new publisher, brought out a new edition of *Pantagruel,* described on the title page as "augmented and revised." The alterations, however, were insignificant, and the volume was carelessly printed. Nevertheless, its success was such that four pirated editions from other presses appeared promptly.

So alluring a book could not fail to attract the attention of the doctors of the Sorbonne, and it was put on the Index on the basis of obscenity. And not without some justification. The work of François Rabelais is marred by obscene spots which add nothing to its literary value or to humor. They have been the reason for alienating generations of potential readers, and in particular women, who, in the final count, are not only the mothers of men but the mothers of reputations. Rabelais disowned women, and the feeling has been mutual.

According to available record Rabelais' patients were all males; he seems not to have treated a woman. And he writes: "As far as I am concerned, I know nothing, and care less, about any female," which likely is the braggadocio of the male proclaiming his superiority, for we acquire importance by denigrating others, and should not be taken *ad literam*. However, Rabelais had spent many of his early years in monasteries where, in order to quench passion, the inmates were taught to imagine woman in her ugliest postures and nastiest attitudes, a veritable vessel of iniquity. He never fully unlearned this vivid teaching, and there was always the whiff of incense about him. Nevertheless, like most ecclesiastics, minor and major, of his day, he had his sexual experiences.

François Rabelais had one foot in the Middle Ages and one in the Renaissance. Never could he step forward freely, nor turn back entirely. It was this, perhaps, that saved him from the stake, but also buried him in the dust of oblivion at various periods of history.

The Renaissance was essentially a philosophy of refinement, whereas Rabelais protested against too much refinement, which was one of the reasons for the grossness and the lustiness of his work—a deliberate childish rebellion. To this was added the practice of his medical profession dealing with the ways of some of the organs of the human body that refuse to behave like ladies and gentlemen.

The fabliaux—those short metrical stories—and the farces equal and surpass the coarsest passages in Rabelais, and Luther and Calvin, who also belonged to the two ages, thundering from their pulpits, used a language that would have emptied their churches in later days. To hoi polloi of the period the "obscene" words had the accustomed tang of the stable and the barnyard, inoffensive and convincing. The Roman Church escaped the condemnation by using Latin, grandiloquent and stentorian, and who could imagine that such a language harbored words fished out of the gutter?

Humanism, the riper form of the Renaissance, had as one of its main tents internationalism, or at least a western European union leading to permanent peace, as seen in the life and work of Erasmus, its most brilliant exponent. Rabelais, on the other hand, was a nationalist, a French patriot who regarded monarchy as the best form of government, although not accepting without qualifications the divine right of kings. Moreover, in his opinion the kings had duties to perform, the neglect of which might in extreme cases lead to deposition. And he speaks of those devils of kings "who know nothing and are worth nothing, only to do evil to the poor subjects, and trouble the world with their wars, for their personal and detestable pleasure."

Rabelais disapproved of wars of conquest, for "the time has gone by for conquering kingdoms to the loss of our nearest Christian brother; it is contrary to the profession of the Gospel." Yet he did not reject "defensive" wars, not realizing that wars have almost always been presented as "defensive" to those who had to do the fighting and the dying—"defense" of God, of the country, of the ruler, of the way of life. What army has ever embroidered upon its banner: "For plunder, rape and murder!"

Humanism had roots in scholasticism, but scholasticism was a stench in Rabelais' nostrils. Humanism indulged in esoterics, but Rabelais, of all great writers, was the least introspective. Humanism was essentially serious and solemn, but Rabelais was gay, uninhibited, full of boyish pranks. Humanism was anti-Romanism, and while no one ever criticized the hierarchy and the monastic life as violently and as mockingly as Rabelais, he also rejected Protestantism with its strict discipline and its dogma of predestination, which to him appeared a violation of the law of nature—*Antiphysis*. How indeed could a man who loved freedom to the point of intemperance, as Rabelais, accept the rule of John Calvin?

"Prison or fine for failing to doff a respectful beaver to Calvin passing by in the street; for singing or dancing at a wedding party; for being caught with playing cards; for locking housedoors at night against inquisitors empowered to swoop for inspection at any hour; for a woman on infringing hairdressing regulations; prison for any public expression of deviation from or doubts concerning dogma, and the liability to be burned for heresy."

Nevertheless, Rabelais was a Humanist, even though a nonconformist, deriving much of his knowledge and wisdom from the Latins and the Greeks, and his literary

postures from Lucian (A.D. 120-180), star of the Silver
Age of Hellenic letters, for which his enemies mocked
him as "the ape of Lucian."

There is much that is enigmatic in the personality of
François Rabelais, even when the details of a period
of his life are known, but there are many lacunae, and
much is guess work, largely derived from what seems
autobiographic in his work.

While it is true that every character an author creates
is a facet of himself, and his adventures are also his
own, since no one can crawl out of his skin, yet the
author transforms himself as the needs of his story require, and the adventures become unrecognizable, un-
remembered incidents. An author is a chameleon changing colors, but which color is the original, no one knows,
not even himself, and the critic and the biographer choose
that which conforms to their own nature and prejudices.
There are also interpreters who mingle all the colors in
an effort at impartiality and totality, but the result is
often a shapeless and bewildering creation.

Yet the author could have done no better had he
attempted to present himself whole and undisguised to
the generations that would follow. The inscription on
the Delphic Temple—*Gnothi Seauton*—Know Thyself—
is an ingenuous admonition in a world in which everything flows—*Panta rhei*—and no one can bathe twice in
the same river, since both the river and himself change,
even while those on shore watch and change as well.
Impermanence is the only truth, and all things are ever
new under the sun, including the sun itself.

And so François Rabelais, Doctor of Medicine and
Writer Extraordinary, is all things to all men.

By now Rabelais began to understand the nature and
scope of his novel, and he set about to rewrite it and
organize it into a more or less logical and definitive form.
Pantagruel, whom he made the son of Gargantua, and

whose story he had written before that of Gargantua, he now called *Book Second,* and *Gargantua,* only partially based on the ancient legend, he called *Book First,* as it was reasonable, the Father antedating the Son. And so it has remained in the History of World Letters.

10

BOOK FIRST

The Most Horrific Life
of the
GREAT GARGANTUA
Father of Pantagruel
Composed in the Days of Old
By M. Alcofribas
Abstractor of Quintessence
BOOK FULL OF PANTAGRUELISM
On Sale at Lyons,
At François Juste's
Opposite Our Lady of Comfort
M.D. XLII

To The Readers

My friends, who are about to read this book,
Please rid yourselves of every predilection;
You'll find no scandal, if you do not look,
For it contains no evil or infection.
True, you'll discover, upon close inspection,
It teaches little, except how to laugh:
The best of arguments; the rest is chaff,
Viewing the grief that threatens your brief span;
For smiles, not tears, make the better autograph,
Because to laugh is natural to man.
LIVE JOYOUSLY!

85

Author's Prologue

*M*ost illustrious Drinkers, and you, most precious Syphilitics, for it is to you, not to others, that my writings are dedicated. . . . Have you ever seen a dog falling upon a marrow-bone? If you have observed him, you must have noticed with what devotion he watches that bone, with what care he guards it, with what fervor he holds on to it, with what prudence he bites into it, with what affection he breaks it, with what diligence he sucks it. What leads him to do this? What is the hope beyond his effort? What does he expect to gain? Nothing more than a little marrow. It is true that this little is more delicious than large quantities of any other kind of meat, for the reason that marrow is a form of nourishment which nature has worked out to perfection.

Following the dog's example, you will have to be wise in sniffing, smelling, and estimating these fine and meaty books; swiftness in the chase and boldness in the attack are what is called for; after which, by careful reading and frequent meditation, you should break the bone and suck the marrow in the certain hope that you will be rendered prudent and valorous by such a reading; for in the course of it you will find things of quite a different taste and a doctrine more abstruse that shall reveal to you most high sacraments and the horrific mysteries in what concerns our religion, as well as the state and our political and economic life. . . .

And now, my dears, hop to it, and gaily read the rest, wholly at your bodies' ease and to the profit of your loins. But listen, donkey-faced—may a chancre lame you!—remember to drink a health to me, and I will pledge you on the spot.

Grandgousier, Pantagruel's granddad, was a jolly

good fellow, a hearty drinker, who, when he became of manly age, married Gargamelle, daughter of the King of Butterflies, a pretty wench with a good mug on her. And they did what young married couples have the habit of doing, and she became pregnant with a fine son, and carried him up to the eleventh month, when he made his entrance into the world through her left ear.

You do not believe this because it does not seem likely? "For this reason alone you ought to believe it, in perfect faith, since the Sorbonnists say that faith lies in believing things that possess no appearance of likelihood."

They had as a most worthy exemplar, Tertullian (160-250), native of Carthage. He became the leader of a sect called after him Tertullianists. He created Christian Latin literature, of which he is the most fecund, original and powerful genius. And Tertullian said, as the kernel of all faith forever: *"Credo quia absurdum"*—I believe because it is absurd.

The infant, instead of crying "mie-mie—," like other newly born humans, brayed out: "A drink! A drink! A drink!" And because he had so big and nimble a throat, his father named him Gargantua—onomatopoeia for *"Que grand tu as"*—*le gossier*—the gullet!

They set aside seventeen thousand nine hundred cows for the baby's ordinary milk diet, and when he was a year and ten months old, they made him a fine oxcart to lug him about. To dress him, for his doublet, they took eight hundred thirteen ells of white satin and for his laces fifteen hundred nine and a half dogskins; for his breeches eleven hundred five and a third ells of striped columns, scalloped in the rear, in order not to overheat the loins; for his shoes four hundred six ells of bright-blue velvet; for their soles eleven hundred brown cowhides, shaped like a codfish's tail; for his bonnet three hundred two and a quarter ells of white

velvet; for his plume a great handsome blue pelican
feather from the land of the savage Hircanians; for
his emblem he had, in the form of a gold plate weighing
more than forty-five pounds, a suitable enameled device
portraying a human body with two heads, four arms,
four feet and two behinds; for his gloves they took
sixteen hobgoblins' skins with three werewolf hides to
embroider them.

There are many more details, including some which
would make schoolboys roar with laughter and bore
those who have passed the age of ornamenting the walls
of public latrines with images of desire and verses writ
in manure. As for the ladies, if it is still customary to
blush, their cheeks would turn the color of beet, which
is a pleasure to behold.

Yet there is much more to it, for the descriptions are
embroidered with vast scholarship and scorching satire
against the prejudices of Rabelais' day, some of which
are still flourishing, since the acid of time corrodes truths,
but adds a protective layer of reverence to falsehoods.
Prejudice is the shrewdest of mathematicians. Whatever
it adds, subtracts, multiplies or divides, the result is always as anticipated. It devours thorny reason, but experiences no indigestion. It lays its eggs in the nest of
truth and its offspring learn to imitate its tunes. Mankind
dances to them, and pays the pipers in coins of blood and
destruction.

Gargantua is a precocious kid, particularly in matters
of *merde* and *cul,* and Grandgousier, his father, ravished
with admiration, wants him to be as well instructed as
possible according to his ability, which seems to come
from some divinity. For this purpose, he turns him over
to the great Doctor of Theology, Maître Tubal Holo-
ferne and later to Maître Jobelin Bridé, who give him

the kind of instruction that Rabelais had received in the monasteries.

Many years does Gargantua spend mastering the futile, preposterous stuff, and as proof of his achievement he recites everything backward. "Finally he became so learned that he never had one baked his equal in the oven."

Thus François Rabelais had his revenge on the ignorant and nasty monks who had annoyed him and on the Sorbonnists who were ever at his heels with lighted torches. In the matter of education, Rabelais was utterly on the side of the New Learning, sweeping away the debris of the Middle Ages. Indeed, he went farther in this than most of the Humanists, who could not rid themselves completely of their early training, and who found in the mustiness of the old tomes some nourishing pabulum still.

"At last Grandgousier perceived that although his son studied very hard and spent all of his time at it, he was becoming a fool, a ninny, a dreamer and a dunce. And the poor man was told that it would be better for Gargantua to learn nothing at all than to spend his time reading such books under such teachers, for the scholarship of the latter was but stupidity and their wisdom but puffery, and such pedagogues merely bastardized good and noble minds and utterly corrupted the flower of youth."

No longer hiding within the laughter of pornography and scatology or beneath the barbs of satire, François Rabelais now made his pronouncement *ex cathedra,* and let the mastiffs bark and show their glowing fangs. And they did.

Grandgousier, anxious to give his son the highest type of education, now engaged the pedagogue Ponocrates, and ordered him to take Gargantua to Paris to find out what the youth of France were studying.

Upon a mare that was the largest and most enormous ever seen, as well as the most monstrous, the size of six elephants, with a horrible tail as big as the pillar of Saint Mars, Gargantua made his entry into the greatest, the most cosmopolitan capital of Europe.

It must be acknowledged that Gargantua's manners at this period of his life were atrocious. Because the Parisians were by nature so curious that a juggler, a pardon-peddler, a mule with bells made them gape in wonderment, and of course his own presence caused a sensation, he was determined to teach them a lesson, the world being a school with teachers and no pupils, everybody teaching and no one learning, and all having their bottoms whipped.

Thereupon Gargantua climbed to the towers of the Cathedral of Notre-Dame and drenched all the spectators with such a bitter deluge of urine that he drowned two hundred sixty thousand four hundred eighteen, not counting women and children. "A certain number escaped this doughty pisser by lightness of foot."

Not content, Gargantua grabbed the great bells in the towers and used them as jingle-bells for his mare's neck. Loading her down with *fromage de Brie* and fresh herrings for his father, he proceeded homeward.

Now, the Parisians were very anxious to get their bells back and appointed Master Janotus de Bragmardo, the most efficient of the theologians, to go to the lodging of Gargantua and plead for their return.

Using vitriol for ink Rabelais ridicules the pedantry of the Sorbonnists and their macaronic Latin. "Reason!" Janotus exclaims, summarizing theology and scholasticism, "we never use it here!" Nor is justice to be expected, for the cases pending before the tribunal are never adjudicated, and thus is verified the inscription at

Delphi: "Misery is the companion of lawsuits. They who go to law are wretched, for the reason that they will die before they get the rights for which they are suing."

This is the ultimate verdict of François Rabelais, student of jurisprudence and son of a prominent advocate. He knows that justice is the compromise of many injustices, and that justice postponed is injustice triumphant. He knows that the sensitive man feels injustice less onerous than the vain boasts of justice by those in power, and that most injustices are committed in the name of justice. He knows how often guilt is the gravedigger to innocence, and that sheep for justice are wolves for injustice.

Maître François Rabelais was as great a teacher as he was a physician. Using Gargantua as model he would show the monkish tribe and the rest of the world what education should be. But before one could begin to learn it was imperative to unlearn, for the good teacher, like the good gardener, not only planted flowers, but also plucked weeds. Only those capable of forgetting were capable of learning. As in the economy of the body elimination was as important as nourishment.

Yet it must be remembered always that the plane removed the splinters but did not alter the quality of the wood, and gargling with pebbles gave no assurance of becoming a Demosthenes. Education might only result in training to express more eloquently one's prejudices, as was the case with the Sophists of ancient days and the theologians of the present.

Truth and virtue, therefore, must be uppermost in the mind of the teacher, who should be able to arouse enthusiasm in the breast of the pupil, since cold iron might be broken but not shaped.

The basis of Rabelaisian education was that rarest wisdom falsely called *common* sense—an amalgam of books, observation of man and of nature, and physical exercise to keep the body fit—*mens sana in corpore sano* —a healthy mind in a healthy body. Not only did Rabelais discard the medieval method based largely upon memorization, but also the program of early Humanism, which confined itself chiefly in collecting and classifying the works of the Latins and the Greeks.

Rabelais was always the physician and the scientist dealing with realities. Pupils should be required to touch and manipulate things. They should visit shops and factories and laboratories, and learn how apothecaries combined drugs; how clockmakers put the minute wheels into place; how printers set manuscripts. They should gaze and report on the face of the sky, make notes of the comets, if any, and of the figuration, situation, aspect, oppositions and conjunctions of the stars. They should go into fields and forests and learn to recognize and catalogue plants and flowers, compare their own findings with those accepted by botanists, and consider nothing sacrosanct save the truth, even if it conflicted with the pronouncements of those in authority, ancient and modern.

Generations were to pass before the training of the body in France and in most other countries would play so important a role in the education of the youth as that in the curriculum of Rabelais, until finally it would supersede that of the mind, and the institutions of higher learning would be transformed into fashionable clubs and marriage marts.

Gargantua quickly unlearned the silly stuff he had been taught by his first two teachers, stars of the Sorbonne, and accommodated himself to the new master, Ponocrates, a sort of combination of Socrates and Rabelais. While at first the work was arduous, it finally became so light, so pleasant, so altogether delightful that it was more like a king's sport than a student's curriculum. And

what was more important still, from the point of view of
Rabelais, any young fellow endowed with native good
sense could have done as well. He was not interested in
teaching giants, but human beings, and Gargantua was
on the road of becoming a man, although now and then,
Rabelais, having in mind his patients for whom he was
writing, in order to make them laugh, would show him
as a giant. "To develop his muscles, they made a pair
of salmon-shaped lead pieces, each weighing 870,000
pounds, to which he gave the name of *halteres* or dumb-
bells. He would lift one of these in each hand, raise the
two above his head, and hold them there, without moving for three-quarters of an hour or more, which is an
inimitable feat of strength." And the sick, helpless as
little children, and expected to acquire their mentality,
laughed and their good doctor joined them. *O tempora!*
O mores! Où sont les docteurs d'antan?

However, soon after, Gargantua is seen playing with
normal youngsters on an equal basis, and his teacher,
who had shrunken to the size of a flea in comparison
with him, is once again his master.

About this time, while Rabelais was rewriting the
Chronicle of Gargantua, he was caught with nostalgia,
or perhaps was flushed with the hope of "touching" his
pater for a little cash, of which he was ever in need and
took a trip to "my own cow country, in La Devinière."

When he reached the place, he found it in the midst of
a great upheaval—a peasants' dispute, followed by a
brawl, stupid and vicious. Gaucher de Sainte-Marthe,
owner of several estates, royal councilor and physician-
in-ordinary to the King, for his own pleasure and profit,
built a double row of stakes across the river Loire, seriously interfering with navigation. The inhabitants of the
village of Seuilly, headed by Rabelais' father, Antoine,
the big man of the district, rose against him and the
"war" ensued.

To François, physician, traveler, author, the situation seemed ludicrous, yet at the same time a miniature reflection of the great wars between nations, irrational and cruel. The incident gave him the opportunity to invent "The Cake-Peddlers' War," which became the core of his story, amusing and ironic, and ending with a profound moral lesson on the folly of conflicts and the wisdom of magnanimity toward the defeated enemy, as well as the emergence of Gargantua and his father Grandgousier, as men of character and virtue.

The episode introduces Rabelais' most delightful creation, Frère Jean des Entommeures—Friar John—who because of the assistance to Gargantua in his effort to defeat his foe, Picrochole, asks him to be allowed to found a convent in the province of Thélème, lying along the river Loire, at a distance of two leagues from the Forest of Port-Huault.

For the building and the furnishing of the abbey, Gargantua made a ready-money levy of two million seven hundred thousand eight hundred thirty-one of the coins known as "big woolly sheep," and for each year until everything should be in perfect shape, he turned over, out of the toll receipts of the Dive River, one million six hundred sixty-nine thousand "sunny crowns" and the same number of "seven chick pieces." For the foundation and support of the abbey, he made a perpetual grant of two million three hundred sixty-nine thousand five hundred fourteen "rose nobles" in the form of ground rent, free and exempt of all encumbrances, and payable every year at the abbey gate. All of this being duly witnessed in the form of letters of conveyance.

Such generosity could be conceived only by a man whose purse was flat and the size of the abbey only by a man whose home for many years had been a narrow cell. And such a man was François Rabelais, Doctor of Medicine, erstwhile monk.

The abbey was in the form of a hexagon and "a hundred times more magnificent than the castles at Bonivet, at Chambord, or at Chantilly, the finest of the day, for in it there are nine thousand three hundred and thirty-two rooms."

Everything that up to that day had been considered the normal way of monastic living was discarded. Since all abbeys were surrounded by great walls, Thélème had none. Since all monasteries were regulated by fixed hours, Thélème had no clocks. Since in the convents of women men were not allowed and in the monasteries of men no women, Thélème should have both men and women. Since only homely and misshapen women were sent to convents and only stupid and sickly men to monasteries, Thélème would admit only ladies and gentlemen, good-looking and intelligent. Moreover, they were not required to remain monks and nuns all their lifetime, but leave when they so desired. Since members of the religious orders took the threefold vow of chastity, poverty and obedience, at Thélème everyone might marry, be rich and live as he or she pleased, for the very word Thélème was the Greek word *thelema,* meaning will or desire.

"All their daily life was laid out, not by laws, statutes, or rules, but according to their will and free pleasure. They rose from their beds when it seemed good to them; they ate, drank, worked, slept when the desire came upon them. None did awake them, none did constrain them either to eat or to drink, or to do anything whatsoever; for so had Gargantua established it. In their rule there was but this clause: FAY CE QUE VOULDRAS (DO WHAT THOU WILT), because men who are free, well-born, well-bred, conservant in honest company have by their nature an instinct and spur which always prompt them to virtuous actions and withdraw them from vice; and this they style honor. These same men, when by vile subjection and constraint are brought down and enslaved, turn aside the noble affection by which they are freely inclined onto virtue in order to shake off this yoke of slavery; for we always strive after things forbidden, and covet that which is denied us." This is the *cri de coeur* of a man, who although no longer confined within the monastery walls, still feels the weight of his broken chains.

Not only should the relation between men be free and unhampered, but also that between men and God. The members of Thélème have no common place of worship, no church, no temple, but each has a private chapel in his or her apartment. "Worship God as thou wilt" is the only command of the Thélèmite religion. Let no one intervene between God and the human soul, which is the root of Protestantism, and which the Sorbonnists considered sheer heresy. Rabelais knew that where "the men of God throve, the rest were bankrupt."

"I vow that through all the lands of Utopia and elsewhere where I have power and authority, I will cause the Holy Gospel to be preached purely and simply and entirely; so that the abuses of the gang of popes and false prophets who by human constitutions and depraved inventions have envenomed the whole world should be exterminated from around me."

And over the Great Portal of Thélème was the inscription:

> You hypocrites and two-faced ones stay out:
> Grinning old apes, potbellied snivelbeaks,
> Stiffnecks and blockheads. . . .
>
> You hairshirt whiners and slippered sneaks;
> You fur-lined beggars and you nervy freaks;
> You bloated dunces, trouble-makers all;
> Go somewhere else to open up your stall.
>
> Stay out, you lawyers, with your endless guts,
> You clerks and barristers, you public pests,
> You Scribes and Pharisees. . . .

Stay out, you usurers and misers all,
Gluttons for gold, and how you hoard the stuff!

Stay out here, at morning, noon and night,
Jealous old curs, dotards that whine and moan,
All trouble-makers, full of stubborn spite. . . .

Honor, praise, delight
Rule here, day and night;
We are gay, and we agree;
We are healthy bodily;
And so we have a right
To honor, praise, delight.

But welcome here, and very welcome be,
And doubly welcome, all noble gentlemen.
Enter also ladies of high degree!
Feel free to enter and be happy here!

This was the quintessence of the Humanist-Renaissance
creed. Man liberated from mysticism and asceticism, re-
turning to primitive Christianity, unencumbered by traditional forms and ritualistic observances, and finding
life a joyous experience.

11

BOOK SECOND

PANTAGRUEL
KING OF THE DIPSODES
RESTORED TO THE LIFE
WITH
HIS DEEDS AND
DREADFUL FEATS OF PROWESS
Composed by the Late M. Alcofribas
Abstractor of Quintessence

Author's Prologue

*M*ost illustrious and most chivalrous champions, gentlemen and others, you who are so heartily devoted to all the gracious little forms of courtesy, you have already seen, read, and are familiar with the *Great and Inestimable Chronicles of the Enormous Giant Gargantua,* and like true believers have most gallantly given them credence. . . . And if you take my advice, each one of you will leave his task, cease worrying about his trade, forget all about his business, and give his whole attention to these stories. . . . Find me a book in any language, in any science or branch of learning whatsoever, that has such virtues, properties and prerogatives, and I will buy you a half pound of tripe. No, gentlemen, no, I tell you, it is without a peer, incomparable, and utterly unprecedented: I will stick to it through hell-fire. As for those who uphold any other opinion, look upon them as slanderers, predestinators, impostors and seducers. . . . May you fall into a gulf of fire and brimstone, in case you do not believe absolutely everything that I am about to tell you in this present *Chronicle.*

Gargantua, at the age of five hundred and twenty-four years, begot his son Pantagruel, with his wife, whose name was Badebec, daughter of the King of Amarautes in Utopia. She died in childbirth, for the child was so marvelously big and heavy that he was unable to come to light without suffocating his mother.

When Pantagruel was born, who do you think was astonished and perplexed? It was Gargantua, his father. For seeing on the one hand his wife Badebec dead, and on the other hand his son Pantagruel born, so handsome and so big, he did not know what to say or what to do. The doubt that troubled his mind lay in deciding whether he ought to weep from sorrow for his wife or laugh for joy over his son.

"Ha! Badebec, my darling, my sweetie, my little twat (it was all of four and a half acres big, plus two fields, each large enough to plant a dozen bushels of grain), my honey lump, my codpiece, my old shoe, my slipper, I'll never see you again! Ha! Poor Pantagruel, you've lost your good mother, your gentle nurse, your well-beloved lady! Ha! False Death, art so malevolent, art so outrageous towards me that thou wouldst take from me her to whom immortality belonged of right!"

In saying this he began weeping like a cow; but all of a sudden he started laughing like a calf, as he remembered Pantagruel. "Ho! my little son, my cod, my little hoofy, what a darling you are, and how grateful I am to God for having given me so fine a son, so gay, so smiling, so pretty! Ho, ho, ho! how content I am! Let's drink up, ho! Away with all melancholy! My wife is dead; well, by God, I shan't be able to resurrect her by my tears. She's well-off; she's in Paradise at least, if there's nothing better than that; she's quite happy, where she is. She doesn't have to worry any more over our miseries and calamities. That's our own lookout. But God help the survivors; I ought to be thinking about finding me another one!"

And Gargantua composed an epitaph for his wife:

> She died of child, and that's no riddle,
> The noble Badebec, for this is the truth.
> Her face was like a fiddle,
> A Spanish body, her belly Swiss,
> Then pray to God to give her bliss,
> And pardon her—she sinned no doubt.
> Here lies one not to remiss
> Who died the day she passed out.

The infancy of Pantagruel, gigantically wondrous, was even more remarkable than that of his father, Gargantua. When he was old enough he was sent to school at Poitiers to acquire learning and to spend his youth.

From Poitiers, Pantagruel made the tour of the universities, in the manner that Rabelais had done, but he did not study medicine because it was too melancholy a profession and physicians always smelled of enemas. He did not study law because in the school there were but three lousy wretches and one bald-headed legist. He was not as yet, therefore, the peer of his Creator, François Rabelais, but he would catch up with him, become as learned and as wise, and indeed become an *alter ego,* as is the case always with authors and their creatures.

Once when Pantagruel was studying at the University of Orleans and he and his companions were taking a

little afternoon stroll in the vicinity of the gate by which
one leaves for Paris, they encountered a student, native
of Limousin. Pantagruel, in his friendly way, engaged
him in conversation. The student, however, spoke in a
mixture of broken Latin and French, the current lingo
in the University of Paris. It was the type conceived by
Girolamo Folengo, whose name in religion was Teofilo
and in literature Merlin Coccajo.

Folengo (1491-1544) was born of noble parentage
near Mantua. From infancy he showed a remarkable
cleverness in making verses. He became a monk, but
after a few years he forsook the monastic life for a young
woman by the name of Girolama Dieda, with whom he
wandered about the country, often suffering great poverty, with no other means of support than his talent for
versification.

He became the most notable of the macaronic poets,
that is, using broken Latin interspersed with vernacular
words formed like Latin—"pig Latin"—"*écorché* Latin"
(peeled Latin)—a fair caricature of the style of the
grands rhétoriqueurs.

Pantagruel was so incensed at the student's manner of
speech that he grabbed him by the throat and would
have choked him, if the poor fellow had not screamed:
"Let me go, for God's sake! Keep your hands off me!"
in unadulterated French.

Since the miserable Limousinite had dunged all over
his breeches, which were cut in the back in the codfish-
tail fashion, and not with a full bottom, Pantagruel re-
leased his grip.

"To the devil with this turnip eater; he stinks too
much!" And turning for the moment into the *diabolin* of
ancient days, Pantagruel poured salt into his throat, and
the poor fellow died the death of Roland, the terrible
death of thirst, a warning that one must speak the cus-

tomary language of one's country, as Octavius Augustus
once observed: "Avoid exotic words as the masters of
ships avoid rocks at sea."

And so, in boyish glee, François Rabelais hurled one
more rock at the gate of the Sorbonne.

After Pantagruel had worked most diligently at Orleans, he came on to Paris to continue his studies at the
University. And he studied hard, you may be sure, and
profited greatly from it; for he had a twofold understanding, while his memory was as capacious as a dozen
casks and flagons of olive oil.

While he was residing there, he received a letter from
his father, Gargantua, proof that the ancient giant had
now completely shed his monstrosity and had become a
noble and generous monarch—that is to say, a man:

"My very dear Son,

Among all the gifts, graces, and prerogatives with
which the sovereign plastician, Almighty God, has endowed and adorned human nature in its beginnings, it
seems to me the peculiarly excellent one is that by means
of which, in the mortal state, one may acquire a species
of immortality, and in the course of a transitory life be
able to perpetuate his name and his seed. . . .

"It is not, therefore, without just and equitable cause
that I render thanks to God, my Saviour, for having me
the power to behold my hoary age flowering again in
your youth. My own conduct has been, I confess not
without sin, but at least without reproach. . . .

"I am writing you, not so much to exhort you to live
in a virtuous manner, as to urge you to rejoice at the
fact that you are so living, and have so lived, and that
you may take fresh courage for the future. . . . I have
no other treasure in this world than the joy, once in my
life, of seeing you absolutely perfect in virtue, decency
and wisdom, as well as in all generous and worthy accom-

plishments, with the assurance of leaving you after my
death as a mirror depicting the person of me, your
father, if not altogether as excellent and as well-formed
an image, as I might wish to be, still all that I might
wish, certainly in your desires. . . .

"I would admonish you, my son, to employ your youth
in getting all the profit you can from your studies and
from virtue. It is my intention and desire that you should
learn all languages perfectly. As for the liberal arts,
geometry, arithmetic and music, I gave you some taste
of these while you were still a little shaver of five or
six; keep them up! As for astronomy, endeavor to master all laws; do not bother about divinatory astrology
and the art of Lully, that alchemist, for they are mere
abuses and vanities. As for civil law, I would have you
know by heart the best texts and compare them with
philosophy. For a knowledge of the facts of Nature, I
would have you apply yourself to this study with such
curiosity that there should be no sea, river or stream of
which you do not know the fish; you should likewise be
familiar with all the birds of the air, all the trees, shrubs,
and thickets of the forest, all the grasses of the earth,
all the metals hidden in the bellies of the abysses, and all
the precious stones of all the East and the South. Let
nothing be unknown to you. In short, let me see you an
abysm of science. . . .

"In conclusion, I would have you make a test, to see
how much profit you have drawn from your studies; and
I do not believe you can do this in any better fashion
than by sustaining theses in all branches of science, in
public, and against each and every comer, as well as by
keeping company of the learned, of whom there are as
many at Paris as there are anywhere else. . . .

"Look upon the scandals of the world with suspicion.
Do not set your heart upon vain things. Be of service to
all your neighbors and love them as yourself. Respect

your teachers, shun the company of those whom you would not want to be like, and when you feel that you have acquired all the knowledge that is to be had where you now are, come back to me, so that I may see you and give you my blessing before I die.

"My son, may the peace and the grace of Our Lord be with you, Amen!

"From Utopia, the seventeenth day of March,

Your Father

GARGANTUA."

When he had received and read this letter, Pantagruel, faithful and obedient son, took fresh courage, and was inflamed to profit more than ever from his studies; to such a degree that, seeing him study, you would have said that his mind among his books was like a fire among brushwood, so violent was he and so indefatigable.

Remembering his father's advice, Pantagruel desired one day to try out his learning. And so, in all public squares of the city, he tacked up *Theses,* to the number of nine thousand seven hundred sixty-four, in every branch of knowledge, dealing with those points that were the most doubtful in all the sciences.

First in the Rue du Fouarre—the Street of Straw— he held forth against all regents, liberal-arts students, and orators, and set them all on their behinds. Then at the Sorbonne he held forth against the theologians, for a period of six weeks, from four o'clock in the morning until six at night, with the exception of a two-hour interval which he took off for lunch and refreshment. This disputation was attended by a majority of the lords of the Court, masters of requests, presiding magistrates, counselors, members of the Chamber of Accounts, secretaries, advocates, and others, along with physicians and the authorities of the canonical law. Pantagruel talked them all down and showed them that they were nothing but a lot of petticoated calves.

At this, everybody began to go around making a to-do about his wonderful learning, even to the womenfolks, including the laundresses, marriage brokers, baker women, cutlery merchants' wives, and others, who as he went down the street, would cry out: "That's him!"

These debates are hardly an exaggeration of what usually took place in the Paris schools. Juan-Luis Vivés (1492-1540), Spanish Humanist and philosopher, who studied there from 1509 to 1512, wrote: "A boy is set down to dispute the first day he goes to school, and bidden to wrangle before he can speak. It is the same in grammar, in poetry, in history, in dialectics, in rhetoric— in short, in every branch of study. Nor is it enough to dispute till dinner, after dinner, till supper, after supper. They dispute at home, abroad, in the country, in public, in private, and at all hours."

And Pierre Ramus (1515-1572), French philosopher and grammarian who turned Protestant and therefore was murdered, together with another 50,000, some of them men of great distinction, at the instigation of Catherine de' Medici on the night of Saint Bartholomew, which took place on August 24, 1572. The Huguenots had flocked to Paris for the wedding of Henry of Navarre and Marguerite de Valois. Catherine's idea was to kill all Protestants at one blow and thus get rid of them. The massacre began on Sunday at daybreak and continued until the 17th of September. From Paris it spread to the provinces until October 3. For her efforts, Cathine received the congratulations of all Catholic powers and of Pope Gregory XIII, who commanded bonfires to be lighted and a medal to be struck.

Ramus, son of a charcoal-burner, having gained admission, in a menial capacity, to the university, worked with his hands by day and carried on his studies at night. His fight against scholasticism, and particularly against scholastic Aristotelianism, outdid all other Humanists, and his thesis for his degree was entitled: "Everything that Aristotle taught is false."

He wrote: "If I had to defend a thesis or a category, it was my duty to yield to no opponent, however right he might be, but by searching for some subtlety to embroil the whole discussion. I was persuaded that the whole sum of logic consisted in disputing as bravely and as loudly as possible."

Having expressed an opinion, however preposterous, we feel in honor bound to defend it with all our might, and by so doing we may even come to believe it, for we construct our opinions as birds build their nests, with disparate and incongruous bits, and hold them together with the glue of vanity.

One day, as he was walking outside the city in the direction of St. Anthony's Abbey, conversing and philosophizing with his followers and other students, Pantagruel came upon a tall, handsome chap who was physically very well set up but who had been grievously wounded in several parts of his body, and who was in so bad a condition generally that he looked as though he had been attacked by dogs.

Pantagruel stopped and addressed him: "I should very much like to be of assistance to you, but tell me, friend, who are you, where are you going, what is your business, and what is your name? For upon my word, I have taken such a fancy to you, that if it suits you, you need never stir from my side, and you and I will make just such another pair as Aeneas and Achates were."

Aeneas is the famous Trojan hero, son of Anchises and Aphrodite, one of the most important figures in Greek and Roman legendary history. In Homer, he is represented as the chief bulwark of the Trojans and the favorite of the gods. After many vicissitudes, Aeneas, ruler over Latium, is slain, but his body is never found, and he is therefore supposed to have been carried to

heaven, is accorded divine honors and is worshiped under
the name of Jupiter Indiges. Achates was his ever faithful companion, and received as his reward the appellation of *"fides Achates"*—faithful Achates, bequeathing
it for all time to all those who remain steadfast in their
friendship—a most rare condition, for friends change
positions with foes as partners do in quadrilles, and men
sow friendship and reap enmity.

The man replied to Pantagruel in German, Danish,
Italian, Dutch, English, Spanish, Greek, and finally in
excellent French, saying that he was born and reared in
Touraine, the "garden of France," that his name was
Panurge, and that at present he had come from Turkey,
where he had been taken prisoner on the ill-fated expedition to Mytiline.

He had marvelous things to relate, he said, but since
he accepted very willingly the invitation to be always
with Pantagruel, with the promise never to leave him,
even though he went through Hell, he could wait to do
so, until he had something to eat. "My teeth are on edge,
my belly is empty, my throat is dry, and my appetite is
barking. It will be a sight for sore eyes to watch me eat."

Panurge (from Greek *panourgos,* meaning "apt at
everything"—"a knave") was an irrepressible bibber,
lecher, braggart, deviser of lewd practical jokes, mocker,
and at the end of his career an ignoble coward, and yet
"au demeurant, le meilleur fils du monde," at bottom the
best fellow in the world. For who but the "best fellow"
would provide large dowries for "homely old hags,"
the viler the female the heavier the purse, and find hus-
bands for them?

His religion was simple enough—to sin, to confess, to
be absolved, and then to sin again, and so on, until the
final scene with the last confession, the last absolution,
the last rites of the Church, the Devil cheated and
Heaven won.

At any rate, he was destined to become one of the Trinity in the faith of Rabelais—Pantagruel or Rationality; Panurge or Sensuality; Friar John or Action—and altogether Man, and Man the reflection of François Rabelais, Medicus.

We are, indeed, one another's mirrors, and that is why we so often become disheartened. Yet, if we are contemptuous of man, what shall we esteem; if we do not scourge him for his baseness, what honor is left us; if we reject him, what can we accept?

Having related his farcical escape from the hands of the Turks and the numerous pranks that he had played, particularly on women and on churchmen, both species disdained by Maître Rabelais, and many other irrational, malevolent and childish tricks, Panurge was ready to take on the erudite and famous philosopher, the English Lord Thaumast. He was no other than Sir Thomas More. For what reason Rabelais would hold up to ridicule the author of *Utopia,* to whom he owed so much, is not evident, unless it was his infantile trait which urged him to tease his elders, and thus gain independence and importance. However, it mattered little to the Lord Chancellor of England, since shortly after the publication of the book, on July 7, 1535, at the age of fifty-seven, he was beheaded by order of Henry VIII for having criticized his divorce and his marriage to Anne Boleyn, as well as the King's declaration that he, and not the Pope, was the master of the Church of England. His head was fixed upon London Bridge, as a warning to all and sundry that heads were not made for thinking, and his property was confiscated, for robbery is the insignia of those in power.

More himself was not without sin. He admitted that while he held his high position, he inflicted punishment for religious opinions conflicting with those of the Roman

Church, which, while he wished purified, he would not reject. For this he was beatified by Pope Leo XIII in 1886.

In More's defense, his great friend, Desiderius Erasmus, tormented in the depth of his soul by the barbarities of the day, could only say: "While More was Chancellor, no man was put to death, while so many suffered death in France and the Low Countries."

Erasmus himself had now but some months before his hourglass would be emptied of its sand, and he died without reaching his birthplace, which he had left so long since, and where he wished to be laid to rest—that elemental instinct of completing the vicious circle.

But Death makes the perfectly equitable adjustment— the world gets rid of us and we get rid of the world, while our departure brings hope to our competitors, comfort to our enemies, gifts to our inheritors, profit to the undertaker, and is a last sacrament with humanity.

Thaumast (from the Greek *thaumastos*—admirable— one who occasions wonder and admiration) came from England especially to consult Pantagruel, whose reputation for scholarship had invaded the Tight Little Island, on certain problems in philosophy, geomancy, and the cabalistic art, for which he could find no solution that satisfied his mind.

After many compliments directed at Pantagruel, and a vast show of erudition, Thaumast proposed that since the subjects were too difficult for human words, they should carry on their discussion by signs only. Moreover, François Rabelais knew that the tongue was a rope by which a man could easily be dragged to the stake.

Pantagruel accepted, but the next day, in the presence of the cream of Parisian scholars, Panurge proposed that *he,* a mere disciple of the incomparable Pantagruel, take on the great philosopher from across the Channel, and if he won, what glory would redound to his master! Thaumast accepted, thus secretly hoping to achieve an easier victory.

The two men began their gestures, some of which were pornographic and scatological, while others mere buffooning, but before long the illustrious savant seemed in grave danger. He began to ooze great drops of perspiration, and looked like a man rapt in exalted contemplation. With a mighty effort, he rose, but in rising "he let a big baker's fart (for the bran came afterwards) and pissed strong vinegar, and stunk like all the devils in Hell."

The audience began to hold their noses, and Thaumast began to puff like a goose. Panurge placed the index finger of his right hand in his mouth squeezing it very tightly with the mouth muscles. In drawing it out, he made a great sound, of the sort little boys make when they fire beet-balls from an elder-bark cannon. And he did this nine times.

Whereupon Thaumast cried out: "Ha! Gentlemen, the great secret!" And he considered himself fully satisfied. "God be praised! And I wish very humbly to thank you all for the honor you have done me upon this occasion. May God reward you eternally!"

And Rabelais comments: "With regard to the theses sustained by Thaumast and the significance of the signs employed in the debate, I should be glad to explain them to you in accordance with the statements of the participants; only I have been told that Thaumast has had a large book on the subject printed in London, in which book he sets forth everything, leaving out nothing. And so, for the present, I shall pass it up."

And let the Sorbonnists do their worst! Rabelais has told them what he thought of the great learning, signifying nothing, deserving but obscene gestures by a buffoon and defecation by a philosopher.

Pantagruel received word that his father, Gargantua,

had been translated by Morgan to the Land of the Fairies, as Ogier the Dane, legendary Paladin of Charlemagne, and King Arthur of England, formerly had been. At the same time he heard the bad news that the Dipsodes, hearing of this translation, had sallied forth from their domains and had laid waste a good part of the land of Utopia, and were at that very moment engaged in besieging the capital city of Amaurotes.

Forgetting his recent mockery of the author of *Utopia,* and forgetting that he himself was the Roy des Dipsodes, Pantagruel with his adjutants, Panurge, Epistemon, Eusthenes and Carpalim, left for Rouen to board ship and go to the defense of that fabulous country, whose name means "Nowhere."

Within a few days they were upon the high seas. They passed Porto Santo and Madeira, put in at the Canary Islands, set out again from there and passed Capo Blanco, Senegal, Cape Verde, Gambia, Sagres, Melli, and the Cape of Good Hope, put up at the Kingdom of Melinda, and finally arrived at the Port of Utopia.

From the geographic point of view, it is a remarkably correct route, following precisely that of the sixteenth-century navigators, who sought the Indies by rounding the Cape of Good Hope, and shows Rabelais's encyclopedic knowledge and his intense interest in all developments of the day. In this, as in his devotion to learning, he was a striking representative of his age, and one of the chief reasons for his survival, despite definite drawbacks in his works.

Timeliness may lead to timelessness, while the hope of immortality of authors neglected during their lifetime, because they consider their work beyond the measure of the years, almost always proves illusory. At odds as to what constitutes merit in art, critics promulgate the criterion of longevity, the most fortuitous of the elements. Many a weed outlasts an exquisite flower.

The prowesses shown by the four adjutants against

the enemy were such that Pantagruel raised a monument to them before leaving the Port of Utopia. "Panurge, delighted, gave a fart, a leap, and a whistle, and cried out gaily, at the top of his voice: Long live Pantagruel! At this, Pantagruel considered it no more than a bit of courtesy to follow suit. The fart that he let out made the earth tremble for nine leagues around, and the foul air he emitted begot more than fifty-three thousand little men, dwarfs and misshapen fellows; while with a poop that followed, he begot the same number of little crouching females of a sort you will see in various places, who never grow except like a cow's tail, downward, or else round like Limousin radishes." All of these the choicest candidates for the monasteries and the convents, no doubt.

And so Pantagruel was once again the mighty giant, and Rabelais had his moment of boyish fun. Oh, how they must have laughed, those miserable patients, as the good Doctor read his pages to them! Oh, if but laughter were indeed the great cure-all! We are, alas, so poorly constituted for manifesting our emotions that often our laughter may indicate grief and our tears joy, while love acts as its identical twin, hate. Oh, if we but had a tail to wag!

The campaign against the Dipsodes continued and many were the marvels performed by Pantagruel, not the least of which was his urinary prowess, flooding the land for ten leagues around and drowning every enemy. Had his father's big mare been there to add her mite, there would have been a flood greater than that when Deucalion and his wife, Pyrrah, were the only ones saved from the wrath of Zeus, and in their ark landed safely on Mt. Parnassus. The lovely incestuous couple repeopled the earth by throwing behind them the bones of their mother, from which sprang up men and women.

Ah, if Yahweh had had that mare, "who never pissed without making a river bigger than the Rhone or the Danube," in his celestial stable! Then surely it would have been all over with that braggart race that deals in pebbles and boasts of mountains.

And there was the strange case of Epistemon, who had lost his head in the battle, and Panurge who replaced it, but who expressed regret that he was brought back to life so soon, for he had had an interesting time in Hell talking to the damned. "They are not so badly off as you might think, though they are in quite different circumstances from what they had been in this life. Alexander the Great, for instance, earns a miserable living by patching old shoes; Xerxes hawks mustard; Achilles is a scurvy wretch; Ulysses is a mower; Hannibal is a poultry merchant; Nero, of course, is a fiddler; Pope Julius is a pastry peddler; Pope Urban is a bacon snatcher; Cleopatra is an onion seller."

And so on. Those who had been great lords in this world were gaining a mean and wretched life in the other. However, the philosophers and those who had been beggars in this world were the great lords in those regions. "Diogenes was strutting around in a magnificent purple robe with a scepter in his hand; Epictetus, all dressed in the latest French style, sat under a nice arbor with a lot of young ladies, joking, drinking, dancing, and having a hell of a good time."

The grave Dante Alighieri put a sign at the entrance of the Nether World: *"Voi che entrate qui, lasciate ogni speranza"* (You who enter here leave all hope behind). But the gay François Rabelais would have altered *"speranza"* to *"pensieri"*—worries. Yet he, too, punished his enemies, but instead of roasting them he merely made them ludicrous and preposterous, and the rewards for those who had suffered here on earth (himself included for a later day), were not vapory and unsubstantial, but tangible, the sort Maître François Rabelais loved—drink, food, and the company of the learned and the witty.

There was no end to the marvels. With his tongue Pantagruel covered his entire army, and when with his followers he entered the Land of Dipsodes everybody was glad and at once surrendered. Meanwhile, "I who am telling you these very true stories," entered the mouth of Pantagruel, and the people he met there and the things he saw going on would be utterly incredible if recounted by anyone else. Not to mention Pantagruel's strange illness, and the manner in which it was cured, that only a famous Medicus could possibly describe.

And so all things turned out well for the good people and ill for the rest. "And now, gentlemen, you have heard the beginning of the horrific history of my lord and master, Pantagruel, and I shall bring to an end the book. I have a slight headache and the stops of my brain feel as though they were a trifle jumbled with this Septembral vintage.

"Good night, gentlemen. *Perdonatemi,* and don't be thinking too much about my faults, since you are not in the habit of giving too much thought to your own.

"And if you were to say to me, 'Sir, it would not appear to be very wise of you to be spending your time in writing such nonsense and tomfooleries,' I should reply that neither is it any the wiser of you to be amusing yourselves by reading such stuff.

"But if you read it merely as a pleasant pastime, just as I have written it to pass the time, then you and I are more deserving of pardon than are a lot of Sarabaites, moral lepers, snails, hypocrites, humbugs, whoring monks with their big boots, and other folks like that, who have put on masks to deceive the world. For they give the public to understand that all they think about is contemplation and devotion, fasting and macerating their sen-

sual nature, and that their only concern is to sustain and
nourish the fragile spark of human life that is in them,
but what they really do is to have a good time, and God
knows *what* a time! . . .

"I trust that you will flee, abhor, and hate all these as
much as I do; and you will be wise in doing so, you may
take my word for it. And if you wish to be good Panta-
gruelists, that is, to live in peace, happiness and good
health, enjoying yourselves always, never put any faith
in such folks as these, who look upon the world through
peepholes."

12

AFFAIRE DES PLACARDS—
ROME—THÉODULE

G argantua, even as *Pantagruel,* was condemned by
the Sorbonne as offensive to taste and sacrilegious.
Rabelais' insistence that his books were mere nonsense and tomfoolery, for the purpose of "giving that
little relief during my absence, which I so willingly give
to those who seek the help of my art and service," did
not deceive the theologians. They were fully aware that
in the arsenal of man there was no weapon as deadly as
laughter, and that he who provoked it was an enemy not
to be ignored.

Every time Rabelais mentioned "hypocrite" or "moral
leper" or "humbug," they knew whom he meant. They
tasted the urine and found it spiced with contempt; they
buried their noses in the *merde* and sniffed sulphur; in
the broken wind they heard the clap of ridicule hurled at
their heads. Oh no! This François Rabelais, Medicus,
was not an innocent buffoon! They knew where the hare
was buried—*Ibi jacet lepus*—here within the covers of
his books!

Before the end of the year 1532, an event took place
which shook all Paris and made the position of the
Protestants and Humanists very precarious. Nicolas Cop,
the new Rector of the University, delivered the customary Latin oration. It contained a passage expressing open
approval of the Lutheran doctrine of justification by

116

faith, and it became known that the whole oration had been ghost-written by Cop's friend, Jean Chauvin (John Calvin), who had published a commentary on Seneca's *De Clementia.*

The scandal became so great that the King wrote to the Parliament, enjoining it to proceed immediately against the "accursed heretic Lutheran sect." Within one week fifty Lutherans were imprisoned, and an edict was issued ordering anyone convicted of being a Lutheran by two witnesses should be burned forthwith. Nicolas Cop paid with his life, but Calvin managed to stay on in France for a while longer. In 1536 he published *Institutes of the Christian Religion,* which caused his exile and eventual settlement in Geneva, Switzerland, where he became the ecclesiastical and civil head, and proved as intransigent and as cruel as the theologians he had fled. Among the men he ordered burned at the stake were Castellio, Bolsec and Miguel Servetus, the great Spanish physician and scholar and his best friend. Alas, that he who has his eyes riveted on God must crush man under foot to prove his fealty!

However, early in 1534, Protestantism was again on the ascendant. Evangelical doctrines were once more allowed to be preached in the Louvre, and Guillaume du Bellay was sent on a mission by King Francis I with the object of arranging a *modus vivendi* with the German theologians. He returned with a paper of suggestions drawn by Melanchthon (1497-1560), Hellenized name of Philipp Schwarzert, the brains of the Reformation and author of *Corpus Reformatorum.*

Never in the history of the struggle between the two branches of the Christian Church had there been so fair a prospect of peaceful settlement, when suddenly on the night between the 17th and 18th of October, 1534, in the leading cities of France—Paris, Orleans, Rouen, Tours, Blois—there appeared anti-Catholic placards, placed by the Sacramentarians, inveighing against the institution of the Mass, the Pope and the Cardinal College, in the coarsest and most offensive terms. Even the King's Chamber at Amboise was not spared. This came to be known as the "Affaire des Placards," a most disastrous incident.

The King, who had not been a fanatic, and who would have wished to defend his royal independence vis-à-vis the Pope and bring about a moderate reformation of the Church of France, was now frightened out of his wits, and fear brought about violence. The Sorbonne, given free rein, started proscriptions, arrests, trials and actual punishments. Printers and publishers were tracked down, and one of them, Augereau, was burned at the stake. In Paris alone, more than twenty Lutherans were burned at the stake after their tongues had been pierced and their hands cut off. Citizens were banished and their property confiscated. The King carried a candle which had been marked by the burning of a half-dozen heretics. The common people were clamoring for more bonfires, delighted with the smell of roasting flesh.

Under these circumstances it is no wonder that Maître Rabelais quit his post as physician without leave of the hospital authorities and joined the suite of Jean du Bellay, Bishop of Paris, who went to Rome on a mission in the matter of King Henry VIII's divorce. "Long before we were in Rome," Rabelais wrote, "I had firmly fixed in my mind and thoughts a notion of the things, a longing for which attracted me thither. My first object was to visit the men of learning and to confer with them in a friendly manner, and hear their opinions of some doubtful problems which had long held me in perplexity."

They set out in the month of January, 1534, and reached the Eternal City on February 2. Since Rabelais never wrote that the Roman men of learning had revealed new truths to him, it may be assumed that he profited nothing by their ponderous chatter. More likely still, their opinions only added to his perplexities, since we are always compelled to draw conclusions from insufficient data, and although by their very nature they must be tentative, we offer them as final. Thus our minds become cluttered with prejudices of which we are unaware. Still, if we waited to discover the ultimate facts of a problem, we should never be able to formulate any opinion whatsoever. We must, therefore, be able to guess, to improvise, to grasp. We do not have to examine all the sea's waters to decide upon its saltiness. Yet skepticism must remain at the root of our judgments, for doubt is the shibboleth that holds Falsehood at the gate.

Rabelais' second objective was to collect plants, animals and drugs for his professional needs, for he was not only physician, but botanist and pharmacist. In this effort he was doubtless more successful.

His third objective was "to portray the appearance of the City with my pen as though it were a pencil, so that there might be nothing which on my return from abroad I could not furnish to my countrymen in my books."

In this intention he had the assistance of two young men attached to Du Bellay's household—Claude Chappuys, librarian to Francis I, and Nicholas Le Roy, a rising jurist.

So diligently did Rabelais set to work that he believed that "no one's house was known to its master better than Rome and all its streets were to me." But as he was ready to write his book, he discovered that a similar work by the Italian, Bartolomeo Marliani, was already in print. He, therefore, renounced his project, and to his great relief, for "it did not appear easy to arrange with clearness, aptness and neatness my cumbrous and undigested mass of material."

By this time, as upon so many other occasions, Rabe-

lais found himself with a flattened purse, and so he wrote
to the Bishop of Maillezais: "I am again obliged to have
recourse to your alms, for the thirty crowns which you
were pleased to have paid me here are all but come to
an end, and yet I have spent nothing for ill use, nor yet
upon eating, since I eat and drink with my Lord Cardinal
du Bellay, or my Lord de Mascon. But in these trump-
eries of dispatches and hiring of chamber-furniture and
keeping up one's dress, a great deal of money goes, although I regulate myself as frugally as I possibly can.
If it is your pleasure to send me a bill of exchange, I hope
to employ it only in your service and be grateful besides.
I see in this city a thousand little knickknacks to be bought
cheap, which are brought from Cyprus, Candia, and Constantinople. If it seems good to you, I will send you anything I shall see suitable for you, as well as for my Lady
d'Estissac. The carriage from here to Lyons will cost
nothing."

Not only did he send the knickknacks, but the Bishop
entrusted him with the most important business which he
had at the Court of Rome and Rabelais acquitted himself
with skill. And he also gave him news of Rome and all
of Christendom, which was very valuable at a time when
it was hardly possible to learn about public affairs except
by private letters.

Marliani's book appeared at the end of May under
the title of *Topography of Ancient Rome*. A copy was
sent to Lyons to which city Rabelais had returned in
April with his patron. Urged by Gryphius, the publisher,
Rabelais set about preparing a French edition, which
appeared in the autumn with a Latin dedication to Bishop
Jean du Bellay, dated August 31. "You have conferred
on me that which has been the dearest wish of my heart
ever since I have had any feeling for the progress of
belles lettres, viz., that I might traverse Italy and pay a
visit to Rome, the world's capital. To me indeed it was

more to see you at Rome than to have seen Rome itself."

Yet the Bishop was unsuccessful in bringing the cardinals on the side of the King of England. And the schism was provoked. Bishop du Bellay with his embassy was back in Lyons on the 15th of April, but returned to Italy as cardinal in the month of July, 1535, and again took Rabelais along as his physician. Shortly afterwards, however, hearing of a plot to assassinate him, the Cardinal secretly fled Rome, and by the 20th of March, 1536, was back in Paris.

Rabelais had accompanied him until Lyons, where he remained hoping to do some work for his publishers. But Lyons, like Paris, began to persecute dissidents, chief of whom, for the time being, was Clément Marot (1495-1544), poet and valet de chambre of Francis I. He had received permission to return to Cahors, a city of southwestern France, his birthplace, but when he reached Lyons he was arrested, and Cardinal de Tournon, the Governor, forced him to make public recantation of heresy, a ceremony which included the application of a rod on the penitent's shoulders. Marot managed to run away and died at Turin.

What future did Lyons offer François Rabelais, twice censored by the Sorbonne? Recantation at best, and the stake loomed on the horizon. Always wary and circumspect as it behooved a man of wisdom, who considered martyrdom the crown of vanity and egotism carried to its logical conclusion, Maître Rabelais placed himself under the official protection of his friend, Cardinal du Bellay, whose permission he asked to enter his abbey of Saint Maur des Fosses, secularized in the year 1533. The permission was granted, and he was admitted sometime in 1536.

Francis I was now at war with Charles V, who always prattled about peace and warned his son, Philip II, to avoid conflict, but who never ceased fighting for aggrandizement. This time he was defeated and France captured Savoy and most of the Piedmont and Turin, its capital.

Guillaume du Bellay, Seigneur de Langey, was appointed governor of the city and, two years later, viceroy of all Piedmont. He was over fifty, greatly worn, and his job shattered his precarious health. He was much in need of the services of an excellent physician, and therefore invited Rabelais to come to his Court at Turin as his physician-in-ordinary. He readily accepted, for the severe edict of Fontainebleau of June 1, 1540, made it advisable for him to flee France.

Rabelais rendered other services for his master as well as medical. He was the intermediary with several scholars, and his linguistic abilities helped in the drawing of State papers.

In those days monks and footloose priests like Doctor Rabelais had the habit of coming to parishioners' homes for the table, and often remained for the bed, and there were many bastards around. However, the Church, in her wisdom, made no fuss about it, and legitimacy was easily obtained by those who wished it.

François Rabelais was not a woman-fancier, to be sure, but that did not mean that he was a total abstainer. Indeed, as a Humanist, he was decidedly against asceticism. His cyclonic laughter about the anatomy and physiology of sexual exuberance indicate too intimate a knowledge for fastidious abstemiousness.

How generous Maître Rabelais was with his seed is not known with precision, although there are biographers who credit him with begetting several children, but since none ever officially acknowledged him as their sire, it may be relegated to legend.

However, there is one child of his whose sad tale is immortalized in literature, and whom Rabelais named

Théodule—Servant of God. He dedicated him to Divinity directly to make certain that he would not become Servant of the Church.

Far from hiding Théodule as the product of a sinful act, Rabelais showed him around proudly, and he was rocked in the purple on the knees of cardinals, for he must have been a beautiful and happy little fellow. Rabelais, however, did hide the name of the mother and every information about her. Was she a lady of high degree and he would not jeopardize her reputation? Was she a chambermaid in one of the inns in which he spent a night in his constant peregrinations, and he would not stigmatize his son as a mere commoner? Did he consider the mother only a coffer holding his treasure for the period of nine moons?

Alas, Théodule died at the age of two. We do not know how bruised the heart of the father was, for nothing that he might have written or said has withstood the broom of time. But his friend, Maître Boyssonné, poet and jurist, consecrated to the little boy a whole flora of Latin elegies, distichs, hendecasyllabics and iambic verses, in the manner of the *Greek Anthology*.

"OF THÉODULE RABELAIS DEAD AT THE AGE OF TWO YEARS:

"You ask who lies in this tomb so small? It is little Théodule himself; in truth, everything about him is small, age, shape, eyes, mouth, for he is a child in body. But he is great through his father, the learned and erudite, versed in all the arts which a good, pious and honest man should know. Little Théodule would have learned them all from his father, if destiny had allowed him to live, and from the small child that he was, he would have become one day a great man,

"Why leave so soon, I ask thee, Rabelais? Why this wish to renounce the joys of living? Why fall before the day, betraying thy tender youth? Why prepare to die a premature death?

"He whom you see reposing beneath this tiny mound once had Roman bishops as his attendants. Lyons is his country, Rabelais his father. He who is ignorant of both is ignorant of the two greatest things in the world."

13

THE WILL OF THE VICEROY—
MURDER FOR CHRIST'S SAKE—
WHAT PRICE FRIENDSHIP

Guillaume du Bellay served his master, King Francis I, well, but after three years of dogged labor, tortured by the gout and other infirmities, he wrote to the monarch that now he could serve only "by brain and tongue," which under the circumstances was inadequate, and begged him to give him his *congé*. The King regretfully acquiesced.

Du Bellay was too ill to mount his horse and was carried back on a litter. He never reached home, and died surrounded by his faithful servants and friends in the village of Saint-Symphorien, at the foot of Mount Tarare, between Lyons and Roanne, on the 9th of January, 1543.

Du Bellay's death made a deep impression on Rabelais, who had always been at his side. He wrote: "All of us, in dismay, looked at one another in silence, without uttering a word, but assuredly thinking and foreseeing in our minds that France was deprived of a knight so accomplished and so necessary for her glory and protection, and that the heavens were claiming him again as due to them by their own natural right."

With the assistance of another physician, Rabelais embalmed the body. The funeral was celebrated with great pomp on the 5th of March in the Cathedral of

Le Mans, and the remains were deposited in the Lady-Chapel of the Cathedral.

In the autumn of 1542, the Viceroy, realizing that his sojourn upon earth was coming to a quick end, had made his will and testament. He did not forget his loyal friend and physician. "To the sieur de Rabelais, the said sieur testator orders to be paid in addition to his salary and fees, *videlicit* fifty *livres tournois per annum* until such time as his heirs shall have provided for him, or cause him to be provided for, in the Church, to the sum of three hundred *livres tournois* annually."

The trouble was that due to the great expenses incurred as Governor of Piedmont, du Bellay's debts were enormous, and it is very doubtful whether Rabelais ever received any of the money he bequeathed him. And du Bellay might just as well have left a variation of the will that Rabelais, in due time, made as his own: "I possess nothing; the rest I give to sieur de Rabelais."

However, later on, in the execution of the will, René du Bellay, brother of Jean and Guillaume, conferred upon Rabelais the "living" of Saint-Christophe-du-Jambet, in the diocese of Mans, from which he drew a revenue without being compelled to live there. But it was not enough to cure him of his grave disease—"lack of money."

Maître Rabelais always preserved a tender memory of his protector, Guillaume du Bellay, and associated him with everything great, noble, and mysterious, claiming that as long as he had been alive, France experienced such happiness that the whole world envied her, and that immediately after his demise, she fell into the contempt of the whole world for the period of many years.

There was indeed a parallelism between the fortunes of the man and the nation, but in what measure, if at all, he was responsible for it, shall never be known.

To keep the Viceroy's memory alive, Rabelais wrote in Latin (in which such things stay greener longer) a book which another friend of du Bellay translated into French, so that the less learned might also enjoy it: *Stratagèmes, c'est-à-dire Prouesses et Ruses de Guerre, du Preux et Très célèbre Chevalier Langey au Commencement de la Tierce Guerre Césariane. Lyons Seb. Gryphius, 1542.* (The Stratagems, that is to say, The Prowesses and the Ruses of War of the Valiant and Very Celebrated Knight Langey at the Beginning of the Third Caesarian War. Lyons Seb. Gryphius, 1542.)

The book was written in the manner of Frontius Sextus Julius (40-103), whose *Strategematicon Libri* is a collection of Greek and Roman history, famous at the time of Rabelais.

Both the Latin text and the French translation have disappeared. Alas, that through the sieve of time many precious jewels drop into the abyss of oblivion, and much dross remains.

The peace of Crépy, signed on September 18, 1544, ended the war between France and Emperor Charles V, although not with the King of England. It contained vague but alarming provisions for the reunion of religion and for "the prevention of the extreme danger that threatened it."

As if to show what the treaty meant in practical terms, in the spring of the following year, 1545, there occurred the hideous massacre of the Waldenses. The Waldensian valleys lie to the southwest of Turin. The name of Waldenses was given to the members of a heretical Christian sect which arose in the south of France about the year 1170. Their history during the Middle Ages is obscure, since the accounts about them come from their enemies who were eager to credit them with the worst enormities.

The heretical sects before the Lutheran period rested on the Manichaen system of dualism, which originated in Bulgaria, where the struggle between the Eastern and Western Churches took place.

Manichaeism was based upon the theories of Mani or Manea or Manichaeus (215-276), Persian religious teacher, who proclaimed himself the supreme prophet of the true God. His theories were a mixture of Zoroastrian, Buddhist, Jewish and Christian faiths, but fundamentally proclaimed the idea that the world was ruled by two powers—God with the virtues of love, faith, wisdom, meekness, and Satan, or chaos and evil, the two forever at war. Adam, the first man, was engendered by Satan in his own image, and therefore was discordant and evil, but he was to be redeemed by the glorious spirits, among them Jesus. The process of redemption is still on.

Mani carried his message to China and India, but on his return to Persia, was ordered by the Magians or priests of the Zoroastrians, who were incensed at his variations, to be executed. However, Manichaeism flourished throughout the Roman empire, becoming so dangerous for the other religions that, under Justinian, its profession was made a capital crime.

A rich merchant of Lyons by the name of Peter Waldo sold his goods, gave the money to the poor, and went forth as a preacher of voluntary poverty. The Roman Church considered this intolerable. It pointed mercilessly to a religion based upon humility and poverty, now thoroughly corrupted by vainglory and wealth.

Moreover, Peter Waldo had a translation made into Provençal of the New Testament, and his colleagues not only stirred people to holy lives, but also explained to their followers, the poor men of Lyons, as they were called, the unadulterated meaning of the Scriptures. They proclaimed to the world that they would obey the word of God rather than that of man. This was blatant heresy, and the Church began to hound, persecute and torture them.

The Pontiff preached a crusade against them, urging every wandering scoundrel to "carry fire and sword and rape," and every conceivable outrage was perpetrated against the most peaceable subjects of His Majesty, the King of France.

The shrewd, pompous, irascible men of the Holy Church, in the name of Jesus Christ, resented any deviation from their notions, which brought showers of gold into their coffers and vast powers. The torture chamber and the stake took no holiday, not only for these good and simple people, who had the presumption to follow the dictates of their own consciences, but for men of learning who were ever suspected of skepticism, the dread of authoritarianism.

It was a period of grave danger and distress for the Reformers and even for those who merely looked askance at the bloody hands of the executioners. François Rabelais, the wise coward, had the new edition of his two books published by Juste, deleted of all dangerous words and phrases, and in particular any references, veiled or otherwise, to the Sorbonne and its doctors. The word "theologian" no longer appeared, now substituted by "sophist," attributing to those Greek innocent hair-splitters all the evils of the Christian men of God.

However, Fate would never give poor Rabelais respite, and his cunning to appease the "hobgoblins" was nullified by a strange and unexpected incident.

Etienne Dolet, scholar and publisher, disappointed with his timid friends, and in particular with the great Medicus, whom he admired, republished *Pantagruel* with all the passages restored, which the author had so carefully removed. *He* was not afraid to get "too near the fire," why should an eminent physician? And how could one fight the "hobgoblins" if one trembled before them? Poor Dolet—how mistaken he was! Few indeed were those who were willing to fight, and to please their enemies men have ever been ready to sacrifice their friends. Did anyone ever throw wolves to lambs?

Maître Rabelais, frightened, hastened to disown his former friend. He published immediately an expurgated edition of his book, and included a letter in which he made his new publisher, Pierre de Tours, say that "Dolet, out of avarice, subtracted a copy of this book, while it was still in press," an inconceivable accusation, since Dolet had merely to take one of the numerous copies of the old editions and use it for his purposes. "Dolet," Rabelais thundered, "is a monster born to injure and upset decent people!" And his character as scholar and printer was besmirched in foul language. All this about a man after ten years of mutual respect and admiration, leaving an ugly spot on the escutcheon of François Rabelais, Medicus, who survived. Etienne Dolet, however, paid for his courage and honesty. He was tortured, strangled, and burned at the stake in Place Maubert, on the 3rd of August, 1546, on his thirty-seventh birthday.

Oh, let not your heart bleed for man's inhumanity to man, for on the same spot in the year 1889, three hundred and forty-three years later, the City of Light, repentant, raised a statue to his memory! Man is ever consistent in the treatment he accords his benefactors— small stones for bread, huge stones for honors!

14

THE WAR ETERNAL—LA QUERELLE DES FEMMES—LAUGHTER IS THE VICTOR

"*T*ake a bite, Adam," Eve said, handing him a half-eaten apple. "Better eat it all. I had my share. Delicious, isn't it?"

"Hm, hm."

"Adon Serpent pulled it off the top branch for me. He said that the higher the branch the sweeter the apple." She pointed to the tree.

Adam looked intently. "Isn't that the tree of whose fruit Father forbade us ever to eat?" he asked, worried.

"Yes, but Adon Serpent said that things forbidden are always the nicest, and he knows everything."

"He is clever, but he has a way of glaring at you that scares me."

"Not me. I find him very amusing, more even than that monkey who turns somersaults every time he sees me."

"You'd do better if you kept away from him," Adam said sternly.

Eve shrugged.

Adam was still chewing, when he heard the thunderous voice of Yahweh. "What are you doing, Adam?"

Adam tried to swallow quickly, but a piece of the apple stuck in his throat, and always remained there (and was inherited by all his descendants), no matter how much he rubbed. He understood later that it was Yahweh's advance punishment, for he was about to tell a lie. "I-I-was eating, Father," he said meekly.

"Of the fruit of the tree which I forbade thee to touch—"

"She gave it to me," Adam pointed angrily at Eve.

"But you didn't refuse," she retorted. "And you could have stopped me from eating, too—at least before I took a second bite."

"But the first bite already counted."

"I could have spat it out."

"Blaming each other," Yahweh said, "and that is the way it shall always be with you, and with all your descendants. There shall be war between you two and between your sons and daughters forever. I covered you both with veils of illusion, and you saw each other as gods, but you have torn the veils asunder, and henceforth you will see and know each other only as man and woman, and that shall be the meaning of your loss of the Garden of Eden."

They bowed their heads in shame.

Yahweh gazed at his first children, molded by his own hands, as He combed with His great fingers, shining like rays of the sun, His vast beard, scarlet as the leaves of the forest in autumn, and He took pity on them. "Yet," He said, "the war between you and between your sons and daughters shall not end in bloodshed, but in laughter."

"Laughter, Father?" Adam said. "What is laughter?"

"What is laughter, Father?" Eve also asked.

Yahweh's great body burst into a cyclone—"Hahaha-haha!"

And all the creatures shook and howled—"Hahaha-haha!"

And Adam and Eve bent upon themselves and roared —"Hahahahaha!"

Thus was laughter born.

Yahweh walked away sadly, for He knew that laughter was but the jewel-box of tears. And He never laughed again.

In the distance, wound about a great tree, Adon Serpent hissed, delighted. He had succeeded in bringing strife between man and woman. He had been devoured with jealousy (the characteristic inherited by all living things from their Creator, the jealous God), for their happiness was the measuring-rod of his own misery. He was granted intelligence, but intelligence only made him aware of the paltriness of the Garden of Eden, and even of Yahweh Himself, while the human pair by their foolishness became a challenge and a repudiation. So, now they, too, would know the meaning of emptiness. "Sssssss," he hissed joyously, and the hearts of the First Pair were chilled with loneliness, which they bequeathed to their descendants forever.

In all parts of the earth man waged war against woman, and being the stronger and less burdened with sexual tribulations, dominated. Yet he could never win an unconditional surrender, for woman was his mother who carried him beneath her heart; at her breasts he found sustenance and love; her tongue he learned for all his life, all the others he might acquire sounding false; she taught him the legends and the tales which remained the roots of his truths; in her arms he sought safety, and into her lap he buried his head when his heart was sore.

This he could never forget, even when it appeared that he did, for it was indelibly carved into his marrow and nerves, and never could he disassociate his mother from his wife. And their battles, as Yahweh had commanded, ended in laughter. There was laughter in the harem, and laughter in the lupenar, and laughter in the marital bed. And the jests were without number. And there was love and there were tears.

The first part of the most famous poem of the thirteenth century, *Le Roman de la Rose,* written about 1230 by Guillaume de Lorris, contains some four thousand lines of extraordinary vividness and beauty. The fashion of allegorical presentation, which, hackneyed and wearisome as it afterwards became, was at this time fresh and striking.

In a dream the Lover visits a park to which he is admitted by Idleness. In the park he finds Pleasure, Delight, Cupid, and other Personages, and at length the Rose. Welcome allows him to kiss the Rose, but he is driven away by Danger, Shame, Scandal, and especially by Jealousy, who entrenches the Rose and imprisons Welcome, leaving the Lover disconsolate.

But Guillaume de Lorris died in 1235 and left the story incomplete. It was finished years later by Jean de Meung (1240-1305). Its character, however, was completely altered. From the glorification of love, it became a tract against woman. De Meung allows the Lover to win the Rose, but only after a long siege and much discourse from Reason, Friend, Nature and Genius, no less than 19,000 lines.

It was enormously popular during the Middle Ages, as attested by the fact that two hundred manuscripts defied the centuries. And it became the favorite subject of French literature.

Somewhat later, the clerk Mathéolus repeated Jean de Meung's attack, in Latin, which gave it the luster of authority. The original work, however, is lost, but a translation of it into French verse, made in 1340, was reprinted several times at the close of the Fifteenth and at the beginning of the Sixteenth centuries. It started in

earnest the great war of the sexes, known in letters as
"La Querelle des Femmes."

The Renaissance in France was deeply distrustful of
woman, following the classical tradition that woman was,
in reality, a botched man, a fruit which never came to
maturity. The Roman Law held the principle of *fragilitas*
of woman. According to the medical learning of the time
a girl was born only when something adverse happened
during conception.

Theology welcomed that notion and put the divine
seal upon it. Let no one dispute it! And if disputation
should ensue, no master-spider could weave out of his
belly such an intricate and elaborate web to trap his
flies, as the theologian could weave out of the bellies of
words to trap his debaters. And there was always the
rack and the stake at his service for the obstinate.

Woman's humoral composition was, according to the
learned of the day, dominated by cold and moist, precisely the elements which dominated criminals and children. For this reason she was to marry young, since she
needed the constant supervision by man, as a criminal
needed the presence of the jailer and the child the nurse.
The father was anxious to transfer his natural responsi-
bility to a husband, who, adding the passion of jealousy
to his other emotions, would keep her in leash, for by
nature she was inclined, driven by an indwelling powerful
animal, deaf to reason, to boundless lust.

Man has always felt embarrassed by his limited capacity in the matter of sex, shamed by that of the males
of the stable and the barnyard, while woman had no
limits. He could forgive Divinity this indignity only by
making woman the symbol of sin, and his chances of
avoiding Hell by his ability of abstaining from her wily
embraces. Thus his weakness became the symbol of
virtue and nobility, and he could strut about as the master

of the world, envious no longer of the goat and the cock.

Celibacy, as promulgated by priests and monks, was the ideal, the only way of fully worshipping God, and the golden key to the portals of Heaven, where angels are sexless and there is no giving or taking into marriage, as divinely proclaimed. There was, as usual, in all spiritual matters, a practical side, and that of celibacy was the relief from the cursed burden of raising and supporting wife and children, and the immunity from cuckoldom.

Jean de Marconville in the popular book *De la Bonté et Mauvisité des Femmes,* published in 1564, sums up the matter: "The slynesses, ruses and trickeries of women, not only those of ancient times, but also those of today, the wretchedness of human affairs which go so preposterously, that man, who is by his nature endowed with a noble spirit, should make himself subject to the deceptions of so weak and contemptible an animal as woman; and yet she has deceived the greatest figures that have ever been in this world—Adam, David, Solomon, Hercules. . . . Man is thrice and four times blessed, who, having the gift of continence does not have to find out from experience, what a torture it is to put oneself in the subjugation and servitude of marriage. . . . That man must be held wise or well-advised, who of his own will, puts his neck under such a yoke, and makes himself subject to such a weak and fragile sex, when he has the means of doing without them and the power to contain."

De Marconville should have accepted the corollary proposed by St. Paul: "If they cannot contain, let them marry; for it is better to marry than to burn." But then Paul was a Jew and the Jewish tradition never condoned continence and abstinence. The Old Testament considers marriage potentially a joy; children a blessing; sterility a curse.

The problem of marriage remained one of burning interest to the religious and ethical thinkers, aggravated by the marriage of Anglican clergy and the hardening position of celibacy of the Reformed and the Roman Catholic Churches.

The Evangelical perfection of filial duty and of Christian morality lay in placing everything to do with marriage in the hands of the father. The first suggestion that one should marry must come from him, and not only the choice of time and place, but that of wife as well. Marriage without parental consent, wherever possible, was no less a crime than rape.

François Rabelais, whose wife or wives, mistress or mistresses, he kept *sub rosa,* says: "Do not expect those marriages to be happy which you stock together in a furtive union without parental knowledge or consent. The father has the right to kill elopers or anyone who aided or abetted them."

"If any man have a stubborn or rebelling son of sufficient understanding and years, viz. sixteen years of age," says the Connecticut Code of Laws in the year 1672, "which shall not obey the voice of the Father, or the voice of his mother, and when they have chastened him he will not hearken unto them; then may his Father or Mother, being his natural parents, lay hold on him and bring him to magistrates assembled in court and testify unto them, that their Son is Stubborn and Rebellious and will not obey their voice and chastisement, but lives in sundry notorious crimes, and such Son shall be put to death."

And the British Parliament, in the year 1770, passed a law which was the lingering echo of the attitude toward woman in the days of the Renaissance. "All women of whatever age, rank, profession, or degree, whether virgins, maids or widows; that shall impose upon, seduct, betray into matrimony any of His Majesty's subjects by scents, paints, cosmetics, washes, artificial teeth, false

hair, Spanish wool, iron staves, hoops, high-heeled shoes,
bolstered hips or padded bosoms, shall incur the penalty
of the law enforced against witchcraft and the like mis-
demeanors, and the marriage, upon conviction, shall
stand null and void."

They who build for eternity block the path of time,
and Plato has been responsible for more than one foolish
notion held by the men of the Renaissance. No truth is
a monument. At most it may become a stepping-stone
to another truth.

Plato held that the womb is a sort of "small, separate
animal, since animality is recognized by two signs, self-
movement and the power to distinguish between smells.
Now the uterus moves by itself in all directions, delights
in sweet smells and avoids rank ones."

Humeurs salses, or the effects of saltiness, according
to Galen, as derived from Plato, can influence not only
the body, but also the soul. In the case of the womb it
excites it to lust. When the animal is deprived of nourishment, the woman swoons and shows every symptom of
actual death, which is hysteria, the malady of the uterus,
this very animal. " *La patiente est fort decolorée et de-
vient palle et jaunestre, ne se pouvant tenir debout, parce-
que les jambes luy defaillent, partant tombe en terre, et
se laissant aller comme si elle estoit morte; et plusieurs
perdent tout sentiment et mouvement.*" (The patient loses
color and becomes pale and jaundiced, unable to stand
up, because her legs won't hold her, and she falls to the
ground, surrendering, as if she were dead; and several
lose all consciousness and movement.)

There was no end to the clamor against woman. In
1521, the jurisconsult, Giovanni Nevizzano, an Italian
living in France, published an elaborate attack, in Latin,
entitled *Sylvae Nuptialis Libri Sex* (Six Books of the

Nuptial Forest)—*An nubendum sit, vel non*—(To wed or not to wed). It was reprinted several times, and one edition appeared as late as 1656.

This was followed by *Contraverses de Sexe Masculin et Féminin* by Gratien du Pont, Seigneur de Drusac, a vast poem in three books, containing a succession of violent invectives against woman, published in Toulouse in 1534.

But while the attacks and the satires against woman and the institution of marriage were far more numerous than the panegyrics, the victories were not all one-sided. There were men and women who struck back, and often effectively.

It all started with Christine de Pisan, a French woman of letters, born in Venice in 1363 and living in France, who wrote numerous poems and prose works in defense of her sex.

Then came *Le Champion des Dames,* a long poem by Martin Le Franc, and *Apology for the Feminine Sex,* in Greek, by Bouchard, in 1522, which was a reply to André Tiraqueau's *On Marriage Laws,* considered at the time as anti-feminist, but wrongly.

In 1529 Cornelius Agrippa de Nettesheim (1486-1533), physician, cabbalist and historiographer to Charles V, composed, in Latin, for Mary of Hungary, at the time Regent of Netherlands, in whose service he then was, *On the Nobility and Superiority of the Female Sex.* He died in misery and poverty, but whether this was the reward for his chivalry, we cannot be certain. It is well known, however, that kindness is a most dangerous adventure, and that our good deeds often turn into our hangmen.

There was also the *Quinze Joyes de Mariage* (Fifteen Joys of Marriage) written perhaps by Antoine de la Salle, and *Arrêts d'Amour* (Decrees of Love) by Martial d'Auvergne, also known as Martial de Paris.

Erasmus' admirable treatise *The Institution of the Christian Marriage* appeared in 1536 and was dedicated to the Queen of England. In it Erasmus stresses the importance of marriage and places it above celibacy. Moreover, he urges man to seek a cultivated and balanced mind in his mate, which indicated that woman was not merely a vessel of iniquity, incapable of acquiring knowledge and wisdom. "Just think," he says, "that if a bad woman is such a bitter thing, what an immense gift of God a good wife must be." In this he approaches the glorification of a good wife in the Old Testament. "Whoso findeth a wife findeth a good thing, and obtaineth favor from the Lord."

Now appeared the first book in which, besides the arguments of the relative merits of men and women, there was also the language of passion and of the heart. Its title keeps no secret: *Les angoysses douloureuses qui precèdent d'amours, contenant trois parties composes par dame Helisenne de Crenne, laquella exhorte toutes personnes à ne suyvre folle amour* (The Pain and Anguish that Come from Love, in Three Parts, Composed by Dame Helisenne de Crenne, Who exhorts All Persons Not to Be Led Astray by Love's Madness).

And there was, of course, Marguerite, Queen of Navarre, who held the center of the *Querelle des Femmes,* both the literary and the practical movement, toward the emancipation of woman. Besides her Heptaméron and her poetry, she wrote works dealing with the subject of love: *La Distinction du Vrai Amour; La Mort et Résurrection d'Amour; Réponse à Une Chanson Faicte par Une Dame* (The Distinction of True Love; the Death and Resurrection of Love; Reply to a Song Composed by a Lady).

The fact is that woman was no longer content to be merely the keeper of the home fires, but wished to play a larger social role. This annoyed man who in his vanity would not accept her as equal. That was the basis of the *Querelle,* which lasted for a century and became aggravated during the religious disturbances, since the Church was largely responsible for the mistreatment of woman and the denigration of marriage.

Woman gradually achieved her emancipation, until the descendants of the Barbarians, more barbarians than their ancestors, under the delusion that they were the progenitors of Superman, drove her back into the "Kitchen, Church and Children."

However, she survived this violence and history will recount the rest.

While man waged this mighty war with all the lethal weapons of his arsenal of prejudice and superstition, countless farces and comedies were written and performed on the subject and the roar of laughter mingled with the rage of wrath. And the blessing of Yahweh was upon man!

15

BOTTLES

*I*t was now 1546. Twelve years had elapsed since François Rabelais, alias M. Alcofribas, Abstractor of Quintessence, had published his two books— *Gargantua* and *Pantagruel,* which offended the Sorbonnists but pleased a multitude of readers.

Was this the end of the story? Was this the end of the literary career of the laughing Doctor? He was already 52 years old, a venerable age in his day, and indeed his thread of life was short and Fate Atropos was getting her shears ready to snap it before many years would elapse.

Had he found his medical profession a sufficient task and the few bits of didactic writing and the odd job as editor, a sufficient outlet for his exuberant talent? Or was it the fear of the "hawks," who knew his identity and who were anxious to put their torch to the faggots at the foot of the stake to which they would bind him? There was ever the stench of tallow smoke invading the nostrils of men in the heydey of Christianity, and prudence was the watchword.

Perhaps Rabelais might have thrown away his pen if the air had not been rocked with the tumult and the laughter of the great war waged between man and woman, euphemistically called *"La Querelle des Femmes."* But everybody who could move a goosequill across a sheet of paper had something to say in the matter, and would he alone remain dumb—he, the most learned, the wittiest, the merriest master of a mountainous cataract of words?

He glanced at his two volumes. The tall tales of adventure intended to make simple-minded listeners laugh no longer amused him. Grandgousier and Gargantua, two honest souls, with hearts as big as Notre Dame, he had loved and still loved, but he had outgrown them and their antics. Alas, one waxed old and one's gaiety was the last challenge to time. Yet there was Pantagruel, really his own child, although Gargantua "begot" him at the age of 524, and there was Panurge, the rascal, and Frère Jean des Entommeurs—Friar John, the wonderful monk—all his creations.

Now with these three, and some minor ones that he could mold out of the clay of his imagination, could he not invent a new tale, whose chief purpose should still be to make people laugh, for laughter was not only the best therapy for the ill, but also the best prophylactic for the whole? But a tale of men, not of giants, a tale that would at the same time expose the follies and the cruelties of humanity in general and of his contemporaries in particular. He was not another St. George killing the dragon with his fiery sword; indeed, knightly adventures bored him, yet he could hurl his darts of wit and humor at the manifest evils flourishing in the land, and perhaps strike some and clear the air a little. Man, he knew, was the eternal invalid. The utmost one could do for him was to administer palliatives, and he was a physician, and that was his function—alleviate pain.

What was the burning question of the day? (The Lord forgive him for using the word "burning." It always made his skin shrivel like that of the red herrings one bought in the market.) What was it but the "war of the sexes," gingerly called *"querelle des femmes"?*

And what was the "war" all about if not about the

unpredictable ways of that preposterous creature called
woman, with whom man could not live nor live without?
Of her, man expected the impossible and got the incredible. And what was marriage but the struggle, so often
futile, to transmute porcupines into pincushions?

François Rabelais pondered long. Suddenly he burst
into laughter. He had the whole scheme of the tale in
his mind. It must have been there, as in an oven, he
thought, baking itself for months, maybe for years, into
its present crispness.

Panurge—Panurge would be the hero—or the coward, it was all one; the hero overcame his cowardice at
the right moment. The right moment, that was all that
mattered—the right moment to live, the right moment
to die, but whose clock ran with precision? All chance—
acorns might be food for hogs or rise into magnificent
oaks, as the dice of chance decreed. What diamond dazzled as glass graced by the sun?

There was always that cursed Sorbonne and always
the necessary ingenuity to escape its claws. He had it! He
would always speak, or rather hiccough, about bottles—
bottles. He would belch in their faces. Let them think
that he was an inveterate drunkard. Let them think
that *he,* not Pantagruel, was the king of the Dipsodes!
And what, pray, could come out of a mind forever cloud-
ed with the fumes of wine, gurgled out of a mouth forever pulling at the bottle, save foolish, meaningless,
worthless words? While they, men of God, burned only
for words of wisdom, of truth, of justice, issuing from
sober mouths.

In a circus where the audience was composed of mad-
men, only the clown had the chance to survive. Therefore
he, François Rabelais, Doctor of Medicine, would be the
clown and slap the solemn arses of the professors with
impunity and laughter. And they, embarrassed, would
have to join in the laughter—at least grin.

His "bottles," Rabelais would fill with the noble thoughts he had garnered from all the books of the mighty ancients and of the mighty modern ones as well, such as Erasmus and Budé and Morus, who lost his wonderful head because he did not know about "the mask of the bottle," or knowing, he was too highly placed— the King's own Chancellor—to use it. There was such a thing as "noblesse oblige," the illusion that there were things worthier than life itself, and that Posterity would pass equitable judgment on one's deeds and conduct. In truth, however, Posterity consisted of human beings, like those of the present, and their judgment, like the judgment of one's contemporaries, was based upon prejudice, ignorance and indifference. The future laughed uproariously at the past, and fame was time's sole gift—a shadow horse bearing no scrutiny of mouth.

Rabelais' "bottles" would be kept cool and fresh in the well of his mind, and their contents he would pour into the cups of those who understood his strategy and came to share them with him. They would learn the deep secret of life—to know in order to love. And for this they would learn that it was essential to avoid the hypocrite, the ignorant, the cruel; to free oneself from vain terrors; to study man and the universe impartially, and thus understand the immutable laws of the physical and moral world, and to obey them.

And so drink! drink! drink! Drink truth! Drink love! Drink laughter! And that would be the toast to all by François Rabelais, Medicus!

Alas, François, your scheme failed! The Sorbonnists were not deceived. They knew that your bladders were filled with powder to blow up their institutions, and that the bells on your jester's cap rang the reveille to awaken men to war against them.

Moreover, generation after generation of critics, professional and amateur, in all tongues and in all lands,

considered you an immoral drunkard and your "bottles"
filled with the juice of grapes, fouled in the barrels. They
could not break the bones and reach the marrow of your
thoughts, and forgot the reason for your concealment.
In their day, the stake, worm-eaten, rotted in the mud,
and although the theologians continued to prattle superstitions, their words were no longer tongues of flames.
They were free; *they* could write and speak as they
pleased; *their* thoughts they could hawk in the Fair of
Letters. And when did the full belly understand the
agony of the empty one?

Your very name, Rabelais, turned adjective, became
the symbol of vulgarity and intemperance, and those who
used it rarely read you. Yet it did help to make you
immortal, for vulgarity and intemperance are hardy
weeds, while refinement and moderation are fragile, perishable flowers.

Still, the "bottle" scheme had to be reinforced, Rabelais knew, by a royal "privilege," if he wished to make
certain that he escaped the claws of the "hawks." And
he would pull all strings at his disposal to achieve this,
adding extravagant praises for the King in his book,
calling him "Roi-megiste," greatest King, and even in
Hebrew, calling him "Melech Ahev"—King Lover.

Also, he would dedicate the book to that good soul
Marguerite, Queen of Navarre, who, he hoped, would
never read it. She had scolded him, gently to be sure,
for the things he said in his other two books, and this
one, as he envisaged it, would certainly contain worse
material from her point of view. She was a mystic, and
naturally was displeased with his skepticism, and she was
a feminist, while he was not always gallant toward
woman, to say the least. Yet she was cordial toward him
and treated him with much kindness, and he had the
feeling that she was rather fond of him. At any rate, at
this time she was not in good health, and a little flattery

might serve as a tonic—flattery being first cousin to laughter, and sometimes even more efficacious.

Also it was childish to continue to hide his identity when everybody knew who was the author of *Gargantua* and *Pantagruel*. And so, he would bury good old M. Alcofribas, Abstractor of Quintessence, with all due honors, and a tear or two. His new book shall be printed under his own name, as honorable as any in the Kingdom of France.

Due perhaps to Marguerite or to one or more of his noble benefactors, or to the fact that in 1542 he had been appointed one of the "masters of requests," attached to the service of the Court, an office without pay or duties, which however gave the owner some claim to royal favor, Rabelais received the "privilege."

"Francis, by the grace of God, King of France, to the Marshal of Paris, the Bailiff of Rouen, the Seneschals of Lyons, Toulouse, Bordeaux and Poitou, to all Our officers of justice, or their lieutenants, and to whom it may concern, greetings!

"On the part of Our dear and loyal friend, Maître François Rabelais, Doctor of Medicine, in Our University of Montpellier, it has been set forth that the said petitioner, having heretofore caused to be printed a number of books, notably, two volumes of *The Heroic Deeds and Sayings of Pantagruel*, no less useful than enjoyable, and being duly besought and importuned by the learned and the studious of Our Realms to cause, for the purpose of public utility, a said sequel to be printed, he has implored Us to give him a privilege, in accordance with which no one shall print or place on sale any works of his except such as he shall cause to be printed by properly authorized publishers for the space of ten years, beginning with the date of the printing of the said books.

"For these reasons, We, desiring that the cause of letters be promoted throughout Our Realms, for the profit and instruction of Our subjects, do hereby grant to the said petitioner the said privilege.

"To this end, We have granted, and do hereby grant to each one of you whom it may concern, full power, commission and authority to enforce these presents. For such is Our Pleasure, so be it!

"Given at Paris, the nineteenth of September, in the Year of Grace one thousand five hundred and forty-five, and the thirty-first year of Our reign."

16

BOOK THIRD

Of the Heroic Deeds and Sayings
Of the worthy
PANTAGRUEL
Composed by M. Fran. Rabelais
Doctor of Medicine and Sacristan of Iles d'Hières
Revised and Corrected by the Author,
Under the Antique Censorship
The Aforesaid Author entreats his benevolent readers
to reserve their laughter till the seventy-eighth Book.
FRANÇOIS RABELAIS
To the Spirit of the Queen of Navarre

O abstract spirit, heavenly and rapt,
Who, frequenting the skies from which you came,
Have left your host and servant, very apt,
Your answering body, always very tame,
To your commands, and which you bore with a same
And alien feeling, almost with apathy,
Would you be willing to quit that hostelry,
Your house divine, your home perpetual,
And look below on this *Third History*
Of the Joyous Deeds of Good Pantagruel?

Author's Prologue

Good folks, most illustrious drinkers, and you, most
precious gouty ones, it is a fine thing to behold the clarity
of wine and gold *crowns*—I mean the sun. You are no

longer young, which means that if you are wise, you will, hereafter, do your philosophizing in wine (and not in vain), rather than metaphysically, and you will be in a position to give your opinion of the quality, color, odor, excellence, eminence, properties, faculties, virtues, effects, and dignities of the blessed and longed-for wine.

Wait a minute, while I take a little suck at this bottle. It is my true, my only Helicon; it is my caballine fountain; it is my one hobby. Here, as I drink, I deliberate, I discourse, solve problems, and reach conclusions. After the epilogue, I laugh, I write, I compose, I drink. And if the rest of you fellows would like to take one big or a couple of small beakers up your sleeves, I haven't anything at all to say against it, provided that you never forget to give God a little bit of praise.

I'd like to tap my barrel once more, and from the draught it contains (with which from the two preceding volumes you would have been sufficiently familiar, if those volumes had not been perverted and jumbled through the humbuggery of the printers), I should like to draw a generous third and follow it up with a jolly jug of Pantagruelic proverbs. . . .

I recognize in every member of my audience a certain specific and individual quality which our elders termed Pantagruelism, a quality that never permits them to take anything in bad part that they know springs from a good, free and loyal heart.

Having settled this point, I now return to my barrel. Up, and at this wine! Take a good, deep swig, my lads! If you don't like it, leave it. I am not one of those pestiferous German swillers, who, by force, outrage and violence, would compel every *Landsmann* and all their friends to drink, even to souse and carouse, which is even worse.

Every good drinker, every good and gouty one, if he is thirsty, let him come to this barrel of mine. If they don't want to drink, they don't have to. If they do want to, and if the wine is to the taste of the lordship of their lordships, then let them drink up, fully, freely, boldly. They need not pay anything, and they need not be sparing. These are my orders. And don't be afraid that the wine will give out, as it did at the wedding of Cana in Galilee. The more you draw out through the spout, the more I'll pour in through the bunghole. In this way the barrel will prove inexhaustible. It comes from a live spring and a perpetual vein. It is a true cornucopia of merriness and mockery; and if sometimes you seem to be down to the dregs, yet you'll never drink it dry. Good hope lies at the bottom, as it did in Pandora's bottle, and not despair, as in the vat of the Danaides.

Note well what I say, and what kind of guests I invite. For in order that none may be under any misapprehension, I will state here that I have only tapped the barrel for you, good folks, drinkers of the first water and gouty freeholders.

As for the giants Doriphages, the swallowers of early morning mist, let them graze here, if they like, but these are not their preserves. As for you tasseled bigwigs, you haggling critics, don't speak to me. I beg you, in the name of the four buttocks that begot you and the lively peg that served as a coupling-pin. And the hypocrites still less, though they all drink a-plenty and are all of them syphilitic, pockmarked, and equipped with an inextinguishable thirst and an insatiable appetite. And why? Because they are no good; because they are a bad lot; they are that evil from which we daily pray to God to be delivered. And this, even though they do, sometimes, counterfeit beggars.

Down, you mastiffs! Out of my way! Out of my sun, you pack; to the devil with you! So you'd come here, buttocking and articling my wine and bepissing my barrel, would you? You behold here the stick that Diogenes, in his will, directed should be laid beside him after his death, so that he would have it to chase away and swat such corpse-eating larvae and hounds of Cerberus as you. And so, down with you, you hypocrites! Back to your sheep, you mastiffs! Out of here, you whiners; what the devil, away with you! Are you still here? I'd give my interest in Papimania to be able to nab you, gr, grr, grrr! Will they never go? I hope you're never able to do your business, except from lashes of the stirrup-thing, never able to piss except from the strappado, and never in heat except from blows of a club!

After having conquered the entire country of Dipsodie, Pantagruel transported there a whole colony of Utopians numbering nine billion eight hundred seventy-six million five hundred forty-three thousand two hundred and ten men without counting the women and the little children, all artisans of all trades and professors of all liberal sciences. The Utopian men had such fecundating genitals and the Utopian women had such ample gluttonous ovaries, so tenacious and well-formed, that at the end of nine months they gave birth to at least seven babies, as many males as females, in imitation of the Jewish people in Egypt, if Lyria, the Biblical scholar, is not afflicted with deliria.

Pantagruel's subjects, from the day they were born and entered the world, along with their mother's milk, sucked in the gentleness and mildness that marked his reign.

And note here, you drinkers, that the proper method of treating and holding a newly conquered country, contrary to the opinion which certain tyrannic minds have entertained, is not, as it used to be, by plundering, forcing, tormenting, ruining and vexing the people and ruling with a rod of iron in the manner of the iniquitous King Demovore, that is to say, Eater-of-the-People.

Like a newborn child, these conquered peoples must

be suckled, cradled and pleased. Like a tree freshly planted, they must be propped, supported, and protected against all ravages, injuries, and calamities. And the conqueror, be he king, prince or philosopher, cannot reign more happily than by causing Justice to succeed Courage. It should be as the noble poet Virgil said of Octavianus Augustus:

> "He who, as victor, did by force assail,
> By the will of the vanquished made his laws prevail."

All questions pertaining to boundaries, frontiers, and annexations should be settled peacefully, with lasting friendship and good will and without the soiling of hands with blood and pillage. He who takes any other course not only shall lose what he has got, but shall have to suffer the scandal and opprobrium that comes with the knowledge that his acquisitions have been wrongly and unjustly achieved. Things badly got badly go, and as the well-known proverb teaches: *"Des choses mal acquises le troisième héritier ne jouira pas."* (Things wrongly acquired will not be enjoyed by the third generation of heirs.)

In order to make secure the government of all Dipsodie, Pantagruel made Panurge Castellan of Salamagundi, which brought in annually six billion seven hundred ninety-nine *royaux* in certain cash and other revenues, less certain, which amounted to billions and millions of seraphs, those coins of very pure gold.

The new Castellan governed so well and so prudently that at the end of a fortnight he had squandered the certain revenue and the uncertain one which had been gathered for three years. He did not, as you might think, squander it for foundations of monasteries, erections of temples, schools or hospitals, or even throwing food to the dogs; he spent it for a thousand little banquets and joyous feasts open to all comers as well as to all good companions.

When Pantagruel found out about this, he was not at all indignant, angry or vindictive. I have already told you and will tell you again that he was the best little great fellow who had ever carried a sword. He took everything in good part and interpreted all deeds kindly, for all the riches under the skies and those which the earth contains in all its dimensions: height, depth, longitude and latitude are unworthy of moving our affections or troubling our senses or our souls.

He took Panurge aside and gently showed him that if he wished to lead that kind of a life and never to be more economical, it would be impossible, or certainly very difficult for him to make him rich.

"Rich?" answered Panurge, "you, living joyously, gaily and cheerfully, is riches enough for me. Everybody cries: Economy! Economy! But they don't know what they are talking about!"

"I understand," said Pantagruel, "you infer that people of little understanding would not know how to spend so much money in so short a time. But when will you get out of your debts?"

"At the Greek Calends, when everybody is happy, and you are your own heir. God keep me from ever getting out of debt. Are you always in debt to someone? Then you are lucky, for there will always be someone to pray God to give you a good, long, happy life. Since he is afraid he might lose what you owe him, he will always speak well of you wherever he goes; and he will always be getting new creditors for you, so that he might be able to fill his own ditch with another's dirt.

"A world without debts! Among human beings one will no longer greet another. Much good will it do one to yell 'Help! Fire! I am drowning! Murder!' No one will come to his rescue. Why? He will not have lent anything, and no one will owe him anything. No one will have the slightest interest in his burning, in his ship-wreck, in his ruin, or in his death. In short, Faith, Hope, and Charity will be banished from the world; for men are born to aid and relieve other men.

"In place of these virtues will come Defiance, Con-tempt, Rancor, with all the troop of curses, miseries, and woes. And if, after the pattern of this snarling and grumpy nonlending world, you go ahead and picture that other smaller world, which is man, you will find in the latter a terrible hullabaloo. The head will not want to lend the sight to the eyes to guide the feet and hands, and the feet will not deign to bear the head. The hands will stop working for the latter. The heart will get too tired of doing so much work for the other members and will not lend them any more force. The lungs will not lend the heart any more breath, and the liver will send the lungs no more blood to keep it going. The bladder will not care to be a creditor to the kidneys, and the urine will be suppressed. The brain, viewing this un-natural order of things, will begin day-dreaming, and will not give any more feeling to the nerves or movement to the muscles.

"On the other hand, picture another world, one in which everybody lends, everybody owes, and all are debt-ors, all are lenders. Among human beings there will be peace, love, affection, fidelity, repose, banquets, feastings, joys, merriment. No lawsuits, no wars, no arguments."

"For all your fine talk, I have no intention of falling into debt," said Pantagruel. "Owe no man anything, says the Holy Apostle, but to love one another. It is a great shame, always and everywhere, for anyone to borrow, in place of working and earning. However, suppose we drop the subject; and from now on see to it that you do not get tangled up with any creditors. As for your past obligations, I am going to take these off your hands."

"The least I can do and the most in this case is to thank you, and if thanks were proportionate to the affection displayed by benefactors, my own would be infinite and everlasting; it transcends all weights, all numbers, all measures, since it is infinite and eternal."

"My Lord," Panurge said, "my decision is to get married. I beg you, by the affection you have so long shown me, to give me your opinion."

"My opinion," responded Pantagruel, "since you have already cast the die and firmly made up your mind, is that there is no further use in talking about it; the only thing to do is to carry out your decision."

"But if it were your opinion that it was to my best interest to remain the way I am, then it would be better for me not to marry."

"Then don't get married."

"Would you have me, then, remain single all my life? The single man never enjoys that natural consolation which you find among married folks."

"Then marry, for God's sake," said Pantagruel.

"But if my wife should make a cuckold of me, for you know that this is a great year for them."

"Then make it a point not to get married."

"But seeing that I can no more worry along without a woman than a blind man without a cane, wouldn't it be better for me to take some decent and modest woman as a wife than to keep on changing from one to another?"

"Then get married, for God's sake!"

"But if it should be God's will for me to marry some good woman who would beat me, for they tell me that a lot of these good women have a mean mug on them. No, I think I can very well do without all that fracas, for this year, anyway, and be very well satisfied to be out of it."

"Then, stay out, and don't get married."

"Well, but being in the condition I'm in, out of debt

and not married, I haven't a soul in the world to watch out for me and to show me that love they call conjugal affection; and if I should by any chance fall ill, I'd only be treated the wrong way. And if I should happen to become incapable of the duties of marriage, and if my wife should abandon herself to another, to make sport of my calamity, and what is worse, rob me, all this would be enough to make me go out and hang myself or run around the fields with my shirttail."

"Then curtail your intention to get married."

"Well, then, I'd never have any legitimate sons or daughters, by means of whom I might perpetuate my name and arms. But being out of debt, and not being married, and, being, as it happens, put out about the matter, it seems that all I get is a laugh from you in place of condolences."

"Then," said Pantagruel, "for God's sake, condole yourself by getting married."

"Your counsel consists only of sarcasm, mockery and contradictory statements. They destroy one another. I don't know which to accept."

"But, on the other hand," replied Pantagruel, "you have so many 'if's' and 'but's' that I can distinguish nothing and solve nothing."

"With three beautiful dice," said Panurge, "the problem would be quickly solved."

"No," answered Pantagruel, "this is abusive, illicit, and very scandalous. Never trust to it. You know that my father, Gargantua, prohibited dice in all his kingdoms as a dangerous pestilence. Let us rather try the *Virgil lots.*"

Panurge opened the book, and they came upon the verse: *"Nec Deus hunc mensa, Dea nec dignita cubili est."* (He was not worthy to be at the table of God, nor in the bed of the goddesses.)

Pantagruel said: "This is not to your advantage. It

means that your wife will be debauched, and you will consequently become a cuckold. Open the book for the second time."

Panurge found this verse: *"Membra quatit, gelidusque coit formidine sanguis."* (She breaks bones and members, and from fear the blood freezes in the body.)

"This signifies," Pantagruel said, "that she would beat you back and belly."

"On the contrary," said Panurge, "it means that I shall beat her like a tiger if she annoys me."

At the third trial, Panurge found the following verse: *"Foemineo praedae et spoliorum ardebat amore."* (Burning with ardor, in the feminine manner, she will rob and despoil.)

"And this means," said Pantagruel, "that you will be cuckolded, beaten and robbed."

"On the contrary," answered Panurge, "it means that she will love me with a perfect love."

"Since we do not agree on the explanations of *Virgilian lots,* let us take another method of divination."

"What's that?" asked Panurge.

"It is by means of dreams, for in dreams the soul sometimes is able to foresee things to come. The soul, when the body is asleep, seeks its recreation by revisiting its fatherland, which is heaven. There it is intimately initiated into its divine origin, and in the contemplation of that intimate and intellectual sphere, the center of which is to be found in every spot of the universe and the circumference nowhere, the circumference being God, at that mystic center where nothing happens, nothing passes, nothing falls away, and all time is as the present.

"And so, tomorrow set yourself to dreaming profoundly. But you must be careful to rid yourself of all human passions: of love, of hate, of hope, of fear."

About seven o'clock the following morning, Panurge appeared before Pantagruel. In the room at the time were Epistemon, Friar John, Ponocrates, Eudemon, Carpalim, and others.

"I have been at the Dreamer's house," Panurge said, "and I've dreamed a-plenty, and little bit more; but deuce take me if I have the faintest idea what's all about. All I know is that in my dream I had a wife who was young, charming and perfectly lovely to look at, and that she treated me like a spoiled baby. Never was a fellow better off, or gladder of it, than I was. She flattered me, tickled me, groped me, patted my curls, kissed me, hugged me, and then, just in fun, proceeded to plant a couple of little horns right above my head. It seemed to me that I was transformed into a tambourine and she into a screech owl. There's a fine kettle of dreams for you, and tell me what you make of them."

"I," said Pantagruel, "make out that she is not going to keep faith with you nor show you conjugal loyalty, that she will abandon herself to another and make a cuckold of you. You will not really be metamorphosed into a tambourine, but you shall be beaten by her, like a drum at a wedding; and she will not be turned into a screech owl, but she will rob you, in accordance with the habits of screech owls. Your dreams, you may see, agree with the *Virgilian lots:* you shall be a cuckold, you shall be beaten, you shall be robbed."

"God help," said Panurge, "the fellow who sees well enough, but who can't hear a word. I see you very well, but I can't hear you at all, and I haven't the faintest idea what it is you are talking about."

Epistemon exclaimed: "It's a very common thing among human beings to be able to glimpse, foresee, recognize, and predict the misfortunes of another; but oh what a rare thing it is for a human being to be able to predict, recognize, foresee, and glimpse his own misfortune!"

Since Panurge did not agree on the interpretation of

his dream with his friends, Pantagruel sent for him and said: "The love I bear you, reinforced by so long a time, prompts me to think about your welfare and your profit. Therefore I suggest that you consult the very capable Sybil of Panzoust, near Cruolay. Take Epistemon and go there, and hearken to what she has to say."

After three days of travel, they found the badly built, badly furnished and smoke-filled hut of the Sybil, and in a corner they espied the old woman. Panurge offered her his gifts, and in a few words explained his mission. The old woman took into her hands three old distaffs, turned them in her hands in various positions, did other similar tricks, then drank the stuff Panurge brought her. Suddenly she started to shout frighteningly, singing through her teeth some barbarous words with strange endings which puzzled Panurge. "The devils will be here soon. Oh, the ugly beasts! Let us run away! I die of fear! I do not like devils! Let us run away! Farewell, madame! Many thanks for your courtesy. I shall not get married. No. I renounce marriage this very moment."

The Sybil threw several pieces of paper in the wind, and after much trouble, Panurge and Epistemon managed to put them together and read eight lines of doggerel, which they brought to Pantagruel for interpretation.

Pantagruel studied the verses carefully and said: "The prophecy of the Sybil reinforces all the others: you will be dishonored by your wife, she will make you a cuckold, will give herself to another man and become pregnant by him; she will rob you and she will beat you."

Panurge was angry. "You understand prophecies as a sow understands spices. From what you say, it would seem that a man's honor and good repute hang from the arse of a whore."

Such being the case, Pantagruel advised Panurge to consult a person deaf and dumb from birth, since words often led to misinterpretations.

And so they decided that Panurge consult Nazdecabre or Goatnose, deaf and dumb from birth. Nazdecabre was called and he arrived the next day. He made ludicrous gestures, many of them obscene, pressing his fingers on the body and face of Panurge, rubbing his nose, poking his eyes, until he called out: "By God, Master Madman, I shall beat you up!" But Nazdecabre did not hear him and pursued his annoying gestures.

When it was all over, Pantagruel, as on the other occasions, interpreted the signs to mean that Panurge would be married, made a cuckold, beaten and robbed, and as usual Panurge resented the interpretation. He conceded only that he would be married, but not the rest. "Do me the pleasure of believing that never did man derive such happiness from a wife as I shall derive from the one destined for me."

"I never thought," said Pantagruel to Panurge, "that I'd meet a man so obstinate in his ideas as you. Nevertheless, to help you get rid of your doubts, I am ready to leave not one stone unturned. According to the wise ancients, an old man approaching his death can see into the future. Here, near Villaumère, we have the old poet, Raminogrobis, who, I hear, is at the point of death. Go to him and hear what he has to say. Perhaps *he* can dissipate your doubts."

At once, Panurge, carrying his gifts as always, went to visit the poet. He told him his case. The old man asked for a sheet of paper and ink and wrote some obscure verses, whose refrain was: "Take her—don't take her."

Then he said: "Go, my children, may the great God in Heaven keep you, but do not trouble me further with this or any other business. I have this very day, which is the last of May and the last of me, driven out of my house, with much effort and difficulty, a lot of unclean, villainous and pestilential beasts, black, striped, tawny, white, ash-colored and thrush-spotted. For they were unwilling to let me die in peace, but with fraudulent prickings, harpy-like clawings, and waspish and insatiable importunities, kept calling me out of those calm thoughts which I was enjoying very much, as I viewed and contemplated, and even touched and tasted, the blessings and the felicity which the good God has prepared for the faithful and his elect in that other life, the state of immortality. Keep out of their way, and do not be like them; and do not bother me any more, but leave me in peace and quiet, I beg of you."

Once again, ex-Friar François Rabelais took the occasion to satirize and anathemize the monastic institution and the Mendicant Friars in particular. But Panurge seemed indignant and exclaimed: "By God, I believe he's a heretic! Is he, I ask you, Friar John, in a state of grace? He'll get his, by God. He'll be damned like a snake, to thirty thousand basketfuls of devils. He blasphemes against religion. I'm highly scandalized, I can tell you that."

"I," said Friar John "don't give a hang. They slander everything else; if everybody slanders them, that's no concern of mine. But let us see what he wrote."

Panurge read carefully the good old man's writing, then said: "By the answer he gives us, I am as wise as before. He cannot but say the truth, for it is sufficient that one part of his statement be correct."

"What I shall say will either take place or will not, that is how Tirésias, the great soothsayer, began all his divinations," said Epistemon. "For that is the way of all prudent prognosticators."

Leaving Villaumère, Panurge addressed Epistemon: "My old friend, you see the perplexity of my soul. You who know so many good remedies, couldn't you help me? Should I get married or not?"

"Near l'Ile Bouchard," Epistemon answered, "there lives one Herr Trippa. Through the arts of astrology, geomancy, chiromancy, metopomancy, and others of the same grist, he predicts all things to come. Suppose we go consult him regarding this business of yours."

"All right, let's go see him, since you're in favor of it. A fellow can never learn too much."

The next day, they arrived at Herr Trippa's house, and Panurge, after making their host a present of a wolf-skin robe, a big bastard-sword, well gilded and with a velvet scabbard, and fifty nice little *"angels,"* at once entered upon the intimate discussion of his personal affairs.

Herr Trippa immediately looked him in the face and said: "You have the metoposcope and the physiognomy of a cuckold. And what I mean is a scandalous and disgraced cuckold. Truth itself is not more true than that you are going to be a cuckold, and that very soon after you are married. What's more, you will be beaten by your wife, as well as robbed by her. You are going to be peppered properly, my good man."

"Come on," Panurge said to Epistemon, "let's leave this crazy fool. He ought to be in a madhouse."

"Should you like to know the truth more fully, through pyromancy, through aeromancy, through hydromancy, or through lecanomancy? In a basin filled with water I'll show you your future wife, ringing the joy-bells with a couple of rustics."

"When you stick your nose up my arse," remarked Panurge, "don't forget to remove your spectacles."

"By the way, what is your name?" Herr Trippa asked.

"Mâche-merde," answered Panurge. "Thirty devils take this cuckold, infidel and sorcerer! Let's go back to our King, Epistemon."

Still uncertain whether to marry or not, and unhappy about the condition, Panurge asked further help of his great friend, Pantagruel, who decided to summon a theologian, a physician, and a man of law to help him out of the dilemma. They were Rev. Hippothadée, Doctor Ron-

dibilis, and Jurisconsult Bridoye. On second thought, he
would also invite Trouillogan, the philosopher.

At the Sunday dinner, all the invited came except Bridoye. At the second service, Panurge made a reverence
and said: "Gentlemen, here's the matter in a nutshell:
Should I marry or not?"

Father Hippothadée said: "Do you feel in your body
the nagging of your flesh?"

"Very strongly, Father."

"Then marry."

"But I have a little scruple. Little less than nothing.
Shall I be a cuckold?"

"If God wills."

Since Panurge ridiculed the idea, Hippothadée scolded
him gently, and called his attention that everything was
in the hands of God. He advised him to marry a woman
of good family, instructed in virtue and honest senti-
ments, loving and fearing God, whose divine law forbade
transgression and adultery.

"What you wish," said Panurge raking his beard, "is
that I marry the strong woman described by Solomon.
Without doubt she is dead, for I have never seen her.
Many thanks, Father, eat this slice of massepain, it will
aid your digestion, and then you will drink a cup of
claret; it is good for the stomach. Now let us continue.
Maître Rondibilis, hurry. Tell me, should I marry, yes
or no?"

"I don't just know what answer I ought to give to that
question," said Doctor Rondibilis. "In our science of
medicine carnal concupiscence can be bridled by five different means—wine, drugs, assiduous labor, ardent study
and the venereal act."

"I was waiting for that last one," said Panurge. "I'll
take it for mine."

"I perceive," said the Doctor, "that Panurge is well
proportioned in all his members, and of a suitable and

opportune age. If he should meet a lady of like temperament, they ought to beget children worthy of a transpontine monarchy. And the sooner he does it the better, if he wants to see his offspring provided for."

"I will, Doctor, very soon," said Panurge, "and I hereby invite you to the wedding. There remains one little point to clear up. It's really nothing at all. What I want to know is, am I going to be a cuckold?"

"You may write this on your brain with an iron pen: that every married man is in danger of being a cuckold. For cuckoldom is naturally one of the appanages of marriage. The shadow does not more naturally follow the body than cuckoldom does married folks."

"Belly-aching devils!" cried Panurge, "what's this you're telling me?"

"When I speak of a woman," continued the Doctor, "I speak of a sex so fragile, so variable, so changeable, so inconstant, and so imperfect that Nature impresses me as having lost, when she was building woman, that good sense with which she has created and formed all other things. Plato was at a loss where to class her, among the reasoning animals or brute beasts. So do not be astonished at the fact that we are in perpetual danger of being made cuckolds."

Other guests spoke, and all in the same vein, using anecdotes of the ancients and many learned explanations of woman's inconstancy.

"Your words," said Panurge, "translated from jargon into French, mean that I may go boldly and get married, and that it makes no difference if I become a cuckold." And he canceled the Doctor's invitation to his wedding. At the same time he placed four *rose nobles* in his hand.

"Ah, I say," Rondibilis said, "that is not at all necessary, sir. Many thanks just the same. I never take from the unworthy, nor refuse anything from the deserving. I am always at your service."

"When I pay you," said Panurge.

"That," replied Rondibilis, "is understood."

When this conversation was over, Pantagruel turned to Trouillogan, the philosopher, and said: "Now, our loyal friend, the torch is passed along to you to speak up. Should Panurge marry, or should he not?"

"Both," said Trouillogan.

"Ah, ha!" exclaimed Panurge. "And now tell me should I get married or not?"

"Neither one nor the other."

"The devil take me," said Panurge, "if I don't believe that I am losing my mind."

And Trouillogan, whose name means Skein-winder, continued his philosophical jabber, and the dialogue between him and Panurge became more and more meaningless, until Pantagruel persuaded Panurge to take the advice of Triboulet, "the fool," the Court Jester, and Carpalim was sent to Blois to fetch him.

Now Pantagruel, together with Panurge and his friends Epistemon, Ponocrates, Friar John, and others, left for Myrelingue, to be present at the trial of Bridoye —Bridlegoose—who was summoned before the senators to explain the reason for some judgment passed by him.

"I wish to hear all about it," said Pantagruel. "He has been the judge at Fonsbeton for more than forty years, during which time he passed more than four thousand judgments, which were ratified, approved and confirmed. If, therefore, he is personally summoned in his old days, it cannot be without some disaster, for him, who, during all his past has lived a saintly life. I wish to help him to the extent of my powers. I know that the malignity of the world is so great nowadays that righteousness has much need of aid."

The day following, Pantagruel reached Myrelingue. The presiding judge, senators and counsel begged him to sit with them and hear the case and assist them in reaching a decision as to why Bridoye had pronounced a certain sentence against an official by the name of Toucheronde, a sentence that did not appear in the least equitable to the court.

Bridoye was seated in the center of the room. Upon being interrogated, he would give no reasons or excuses and make any answer, except that he had grown old and had not upon the occasion in question been able to see quite so well as usual, citing the divers miseries and calamities that old age brings with it. For this reason he had not been able to recognize the points on the dice as distinctly as in the past, and he had taken a four for a five, since he made use of the small dice.

"And just how do you work it, my friend?" asked Trinquamelle—Bluster, the presiding judge.

"What I do is this. Having well viewed, reviewed, read, reread, rummaged, and leafed through all the complaints, summonses, appearances, warrants, interrogations preliminary hearings exhibits, citations, bills, petitions, inquiries, answers, etc., etc., as a good judge ought to do, I place at one end of the table, in my chambers, all the defendant's bags, and then I give him the first throw. Having done this, I place the plaintiff's bags at the other end of the table, and I proceed to give him a due and equal chance. I become familiar with the obscure point of law by the number of bags at one end and at the other. And then I proceed to make use of my small dice. I have other big dice, very pretty and melodious, of which I make use, when the matter is more fluid, that is when there are fewer bags. I give the decision to the one who wins the throw, in accordance with the judicial, tribunary, praetorian, first-come-first-served dice."

When Bridoye stopped, Trinquamelle ordered him out of the chamber, and addressed Pantagruel: "August Prince, we beg you to be good enough to dispense sentence which would seem judicial and equitable."

After the usual compliments, Pantagruel said: "In Bridoye I recognize several qualities which entitle him to pardon—old age, simplicity, and that his sole error be absorbed in the immense sea of the multitudinous equitable sentences which he had administered in the past forty years, as if in the Loire River I would throw a drop of ocean water; that sole drop nobody would feel; nobody would call the river salty." With this, Pantagruel bowed before the whole court and left.

And Maître François Rabelais having had his ironic fling at courts, jurisprudence, advocates (including his own father, who had disinherited him), laughed uproariously, bequeathed his laughter to all generations, and was made whole. For he had been sickened by the stupidities, superstitions, perversities, partialities, obliquities of those who promulgated the laws and of those who interpreted them. And God, too, was guilty, since He had made man a distorted image of Himself, who imitated His apparent injustices, without having the capacity to penetrate into them and discover immutable laws, their unequivocal interpretations, and utterly impartial rewards and punishments.

Pantagruel was back on the sixth day, and at the same hour Triboulet arrived by boat from Blois. Panurge gave him food and wine and a variety of valuable presents, as he had given all from whom he desired counsel, his generosity being based upon the inexhaustible wealth of his king and friend, Pantagruel, whose coffers were always open.

Panurge exposed his affair in elegant rhetorical terms. Before he finished, however, Triboulet struck him with his fist between the shoulders, returned the bottle of wine emptied, and for all answer said: "By God, enraged madman, watch out for the monk, Cornemuse—Bagpipe —of Buzançay!" After that he would say nothing more, but played with his bladder.

"He is surely crazy, one cannot deny it; but crazier still is he who brought him here, and I the craziest for having told him my thoughts," said Panurge.

Pantagruel, being of a different opinion, attempted to interpret the "fool's" sentence and his gestures. He said to Panurge: "You will be made a cuckold by a monk. On the truth of this I am ready to pledge my sacred honor. The other oracles were vague, without saying by whom you would become a cuckold and your wife an adultress. The noble Triboulet tells it to us, and it will be an infamous and highly scandalous affair, too. Moreover, you will be beaten and robbed by her."

Panurge, of course, contradicted him, and he interpreted the words to mean that he would be happy with his wife. "There is another point which you do not seem to take into consideration. He gave me the empty bottle. What does *that* mean?"

"It means, without doubt, that your wife will be a drunkard," answered Pantagruel.

"On the contrary," retorted Panurge, "because the bottle was empty, it means that he is sending me to the bottle. And I shall not pursue my enterprise until I have heard from the oracle of the *Dive Bouteille*—the Holy Bottle. Let us go there. I know that you love to travel and are always desirous to see things and to learn. And we shall see wonderful things, I assure you."

"Willingly," said Pantagruel, "but before we start out, and we shall make the journey by way of the Land of the Lanterns, we must obtain the counsel and permission of the King, my Father."

As Pantagruel entered the great hall of the castle, he came upon the good Gargantua emerging from the council chamber. He explained his plan and begged his father for permission to put it into execution.

"I praise, my very dear son, the God who keeps you in the path of virtuous intentions. I am quite willing that you should make this journey; but I wish, likewise, that you would acquire a desire and determination to marry."

"Mildest of fathers," replied Pantagruel, "I have not even thought of it as yet. I may sooner be rigid in death at your feet than live and be married without your consent."

"My dearest son, I believe in you. In my day, there was on this continent a certain country in which were found certain indescribable mole-burrowing image-toters, who, while full of salaciousness and lasciviousness, were yet opposed to marriage as though they had been capons instead of priestly roosters; and these fellows set up to give the people laws in the matter of marriage. And the superstition and the stupidity of the married sanctioned and lent obedience to laws so malicious and so barbarous. The victims might with equal justice lay down laws for those mystery-mongers, concerning the latter's ceremonies and sacrifices, seeing that they are in the habit of decimating and gnawing away the fruit of people's labor, the result of the sweat of their hands, in order to nourish and keep themselves in plenty. And such laws would not be so perverse or so impertinent as those the people receive from them. There is no law in the world that gives children to right to marry without the knowledge and consent of their parents. And yet these mole-burrowers consider their own consent sufficient, and they do it for their own interest and profit.

"There is accordingly small room for wonder, if when the father finds the pimp at the instigation of the mole-burrower engaged in betraying his daughter and stealing her out of her own home, even if it be with her consent, that he puts them both to death ignominiously. He may and ought to put them to death and throw their bodies out to be torn to pieces by beasts, as being unworthy of our great and cherishing Mother, the Earth, whose embrace we know as burial.

"And so, my beloved son, after my death see to it that such laws are never enacted in our realm. Since, therefore, you refer the question of your marriage to me, I may tell you that I am in favor of it and will take the proper steps. Go then, and make your preparations for your journey with Panurge. Take also whatever you may need from my treasury. During your absence I will both provide a wife for you and prepare a wedding feast, if ever there was one."

Some days later, after having taken farewell of the good Gargantua, who prayed for his son's safety, Pantagruel prepared his trip in grand style, the number of his boats equaling that of the armada that had left Greece for Troy.

Among the many things that were carried was the marvelous plant called Pantagruelion—a plant with countless admirable virtues, even the ability to resist fire —named for Pantagruel, its creator. *"Pantagruel, l'idée et exemplaire de toute joyeuse perfection"* (Pantagruel, the idea and exemplar of the wholly joyous perfection).

The gods upon Olympus trembled. "Pantagruel has put us into a painful situation, because of the powers of his plant. Before long he will be married and have children. We can do nothing to stop him, for his fate has already passed the distaffs of the Sisters of Necessity. His children will invent a Pantagruelion of such energy that it will become possible for humans to get to the source of rain and lightning; to invade the region of the moon; to enter the territories of the celestial signs and establish themselves, some at Golden Eagle, others at the Sheep, the Crown, the Harp, the Silver Lion; to sit at the table with us and take wives from among the goddesses."

And it happened as the gods had feared. The children of Pantagruel have discovered the super-Pantagruelion and have invaded the celestial habitations, and the poor gods have fled and there are no goddesses for the astronauts to marry.

The vaster the universe becomes, the more desperate becomes the housing problem for the celestial inhabitants. And they who once had all the stars as their vault have but the passing vapors for their roof.

Man has created gods and angels and devils; perhaps the day will soon come when he will at last create man. And when that takes place he will be worthy of Pantagruelion and of Pantagruelism, which means: *"Contentement certain, asseurance parfaict, deprisement incroyable, de tout ce pourquoy les hommes tant veiglent, travaillent, navigent et batailent."* (A rooted and grounded cheerfulness, a perfect confidence, and an incredible contempt for all trifles for the sake of which men watch, toil, navigate and fight.)

A religion this of experimentation and of social *ataraxia,* the Greek "calmness of mind," to counteract vanity and self-conceit. A religion of unconquerable good temper and heroic enjoyment. A religion without temples, without priests, and even without God, unless He be identified with Nature. *"Deus sive Natura"*—God or Nature, as the great Jewish philosopher of Holland would have it.

Thus *Book Third,* the most fascinating, the most erudite, the most amusing of Doctor François Rabelais' work, ends with an enigma and a mystery, as all good things must end.

And he became known as one of the most notorious, dangerous and typical enemies of the feminine sex. In reality, however, he was also satirizing masculine jealousy, inadequacy, pretentiousness, and the unwillingness to base marriage upon real companionship.

And the "Battle of the Sexes," as it was devised in the Garden of Eden was tempered in the cooling waters of the Sea of Laughter.

17

THE SOUL IS AN ASS—CHAMBRE ARDENTE—NAUMACHIA AND SCIOMACHIA—SORBONNE VERSUS ROYAL PRIVILEGE

*T*he year 1546 was a painful and somber one for France. Francis I, uneasy and poor in health, could not withstand the savage demands of the Sorbonne and of the Parliament, and Humanists, poets, philosophers, scholars, publishers, printers were all in grave peril if suspected of favoring the Reformation of the Church, or seemed tolerant toward Lutherism.

Clement Marot was dragging out his days in poverty and exile. Bonaventure Desperiers had committed suicide. Etienne Dolet was tortured, hanged and burned. At Meaux, the cradle of the gentlest Reformers, fourteen stakes were lighted.

In this melancholy atmosphere, in the smoke dripping with the fat of human bodies, *Book Third of the Heroic Deeds and Sayings of the Worthy Pantagruel, Composed by M. Fran. Rabelais, Doctor of Medicine* appeared, published by Chrétien Wechel, at the Écu de Bâle.

Despite the royal "Privilege" and the "Dedication" to Queen of Navarre, some time before Easter, the Sorbonne passed the same formal censure on *Book Third* as on the previous two. Among other things, the theologians were annoyed no end that the word *"âne"* (ass) appeared instead of *"âme"* (soul) in three various passages. In vain did Maître Rabelais try to blame the printer for the "error." The learned doctors would not listen. They knew the "Buffoon" only too well. Man's soul was nothing but a braying ass to him. Had he not dissected human bodies publicly, unconcerned about what might have happened to the soul, which, perhaps, had as yet been unable to extricate itself from the web of tripe and muscle and nerve? That was the reason for their irrevocable decree against cutting corpses, not because of their reverence for the body, as many erroneously imagined. But, of course, Rabelais' dissections took place at Montpellier, that University which still stank of the Jews who had founded it. They who killed God, would they mind the agony of a human soul, and even its death?

All the world of flesh was illusion, and only the soul had reality, and he who dared make sport of it, calling it "ass," must be silenced and his pen broken, that he himself in flames achieve divine forgiveness.

And M. Fran. Rabelais, Medicus, beginning to feel the heat approaching him, fled on March 28, 1546, across the frontier into Metz, a city of Alsace-Lorraine, on the River Moselle, which in modern history changed hands several times between France and Germany.

Rabelais was accompanied by the former Captain Etienne Lorens, who had received him so well earlier in his castle at Saint-Ay, on the banks of the Loire, that he presumed to invite some of his own friends there. "Come not when you please, but when you are impelled by the will of the good God, who, full of pity, never created Lent, but did create salads, herrings, haddocks, carps, pikes, perches, etc., etc. And there are good wines especially held for your arrival. *Ergo, veni, domine, et noli tardere.*"

At this time Metz was a free town under the Holy Roman Empire, so that unless the "hobgoblins" could persuade the Municipality to give him up, Rabelais was unassailable. But the town councilors had no intention whatever of surrendering him. On the contrary, they were delighted to be in a position to employ such a formidable scholar, and they offered him three times the salary he had obtained at the Lyons hospital to be head doctor of their own. He took lodging in a house owned by the Lord of Saint-Ay, in the Jewish quarter, where he was treated with reverence, since a physician had always been regarded among the Jews as a man of the highest caliber. Moreover, one who had to flee the Inquisition was naturally a liberal person, much less apt to be filled with hatred and theological prejudice. In the case of Maître Rabelais this was notably true.

Life in Metz for a French freethinker was quite pleasant. The language spoken was French, and there were many foreign intellectuals, some of whom were Protestants of princely wealth, and the general tone was one of tolerance and progress.

The inhabitants were so pleased with Rabelais' services that the authorities granted him three months' salary as a gratification. Yet before he actually began his work in the hospital on April 25, as always he found himself in straitened circumstances. As he had done on other occasions, he wrote to Cardinal du Bellay, half in humility, and half in arrogance, for money. "If you do not take pity on me, I do not know what will become of me. If you continue to subsidize me, I am yours; if you do not, in the extremity of despair, I shall take service with someone about here, as my condition and station in life demand, to the detriment and evident loss to my studies. It is not possible to live more frugally than I am doing. My Lord, I commend myself very humbly to your good graces, and pray Our Lord to grant you a very happy and long life, with perfect health.

"From Metz, this 6th of February, 1546, Your very humble servant, François Rabelais, Physician."

In truth, the Cardinal owed him money, for his

brother had left him in his will a substantial sum for services rendered, but like the defunct, the Prince of the Church was in debt, since he considered it a sign of devotion to his God to live in great luxury and beyond his means.

On the other hand, Doctor Rabelais had had much experience in such matters, and he knew that in order to be heard by the great and powerful, one had to knock at the gate loudly and insistently, and not blush for being importunate. *"Audace; Audace! Toujours de l' Audace!"* as the great Revolutionist would say two centuries later, and as the great Virgil had said many centuries earlier: *"Audaces fortuna juvat"* (Fortune favors the audacious).

Francis I died on the first of March, 1547, and was succeeded by his only surviving son, Henry II (1519-1559). In 1533 his father had married him to Catherine de' Medici, who later plotted the monstrous murder-fest of Saint Bartholomew. By her he had seven children, all of whom came to the throne, pointing a moral lesson to the immorality of Fate.

Henry was a robust man and inherited his father's love of violent exercise, but his character was weak and his intelligence mediocre. He possessed none of the brilliant, even if superficial, gifts of his father; he was cold, haughty, melancholy and dull. Dominated completely by his mistress, Diane de Poitiers, as bigoted as himself, upon his accession to the throne, he promptly began to apply severer measures against heretics, among whom were included the mildest critics of the Church.

On October 8, 1547, a second criminal court of the Parliament of Paris was especially created for the trial of heretics, the *Chambre Ardente*—the Burning Chamber. The name referred both to the fact that the proceedings took place in a room from which all daylight was excluded and was lit by torches, and to the final outcome of the trial—the stake. It sat continuously for twenty-five months, during which time it passed at least five hundred sentences, and it functioned until 1682.

On June 30, 1559, when tilting with the Count of Montgomery, Henry was wounded in the temple by a lance. Despite the attentions of Ambroise Paré (1517-1590), famous surgeon, discoverer of the ligature of arteries in amputations, Henry died on July 10.

Rabelais had waited for one reason or another, perhaps for fear of the Sorbonne, for twelve years to write the sequel to his first two books. But *Book Fourth* he was anxious to compose at once, even while the theologians were still thundering against the *Third,* and although at the same time he wrote: "I was more than of a mind not to write another iota."

However, the urge to scratch his plume across the paper was too powerful for him to overcome. There is a malaise that only the artist and the pregnant woman know.

Moreover, being in Metz, he was safe, and when he had eleven chapters of the new book done, he published it. His name appeared on the title page, but the publisher's name was absent, although Pierre de Tours has been generally accepted as the one, and the place of publication is mentioned as Lyons.

There was little in the chapters themselves to which the hawk-eyed Sorbonnists could take umbrage, but they knew that the "rat" must be hidden between the lines, even if their noses did not instantly locate it.

Besides, in the Prologue, Maître Rabelais could not refrain from thumbing his nose *To Whom It Might Concern,* and it always concerned the doctors of the great university, which was a wizards' cauldron wherein superstition and prejudice and hatred boiled all the time. "Those canting bigots, booted monks, cannibals, hypocrites, misanthropes, and agelasts, that is those who never laugh, watching all the world in eager appetite to see and read my writings, because of the preceding books, have spat in the basin; that is to say, they have by their handling befouled, decried, and calumniated them, with the intention that no one should read them save their own poltroon selves. They imitated the ill-disposed Greek sophists, who enjoyed free meals by spitting in tavern dishes to make disgusted epicures abandon them."

When Cardinal Jean du Bellay, in poor health, asked Rabelais to accompany him, as his physician, to Rome, he accepted with alacrity, not only because of the danger stirred by the truncated portion of his book, but because his vagabond nature clamored for change.

As Crown Prince, Henry II was a great friend of the Cardinal, but now the royal Court was too reactionary for a prelate with Humanistic tendencies to be around, and it was better for both of them that du Bellay should serve the throne from a distance—a genteel exile in the shape of ambassadorship.

This was Rabelais' fourth visit to the Eternal City, but he no longer had any special object in mind, except that he was ever alert to political and social conditions, which in one disguise or another, would appear for satire or belly laughter in his books. The disguises, in the great lapse of time, have become more or less opaque, but they were thin veils for his contemporaries, which the Sorbonnists were ever in the act of tearing off.

The Cardinal had hoped that a few months away from the French capital would suffice to cool the passions of the courtiers against him, and that he could return and be allowed to attend to his sacerdotal duties. But the months passed by, and in spite of repeated letters to the Constable and the Cardinal of Lorraine, in which he complained of his gout and the Roman climate, he was not recalled.

Meanwhile he lived in his usual magnificent style. His palace was on the Piazza de' Santi Apostoli, those miserable fishermen of the Galilean waters, whose souls in Heaven rejoiced to see how their descendants had succeeded in the Vale of Tears. They themselves, of course, had not done too badly, for in their sanctitude they always dined at the table with the angels, and God Himself would honor them with His three luminous faces on special occasions, such as the advent of a new saint or the victory by uncircumcised Christian soldiers over the circumcised Turks, although in the hoary days of Avraham—Father of Many—He was all for circumcision.

Indeed, it was a fabulous success all around, considering the original paltry investment—a cross upon which a Jew, rebel against an invading army and a perfidious priesthood, rotted in agony, calling out in vain: *"Eloi, Eloi, lama sabachthani?"* (My God, my God, why hast Thou forsaken me?) Avraham spared *his* son, but not so the Almighty.

On March 14, 1549, Cardinal du Bellay gave a magnificent entertainment in the Piazza de' Santi Apostoli to celebrate the birth of Louis d' Orléans, the second son of Henry II and Catherine de' Medici, an entertainment which became famous and immortal because Maître Rabelais was both the author of some mechanical contrivances and the author of a book describing the events.

The *pièce de résistance* took the shape of spectacular sham battles in the fashionable Renaissance style—a *naumachia* or mock sea battle, staged on the Tiber, and a *sciomachia* or mock land battle, fought four days later on the Piazza.

The Tiber, unfortunately, being in flood, spoiled that aquatic spectacle, but the land one proved very successful, and Rabelais was engaged by the Cardinal to describe it in detail for the delectation of the French Court.

A great wooden castle was created in the Piazza and there were attackers and defenders—three hundred infantry troops and fifty cavalrymen. And there were fife and drum and hautboys and flutes, for the recovery of Goddess Diana and her attending hunting nymphs who had been "kidnapped" by a party of roving soldiers.

This was followed by a sumptuous supper at which were imbibed thirty puncheons of wine, each containing a hundred gallons, and devoured "a myriad varieties of fish, and more than five hundred different oven products, by which I mean pastries, tarts, and the like and one hundred fifty dozen loaves of bread."

There was a performance of Spanish dancers, and several masks, and finally a ball which lasted till daylight, "when the most reverend lords, the ambassadors, and other prelates, retired with great jubilation and content. The house of my Most Reverend Lord was open to all comers, no matter who. *"Ouverte à tous venans, quelz qu'ils fussent."*

"As for the banquet," Rabelais further writes, "I observed two singular things: in the first place, there was no discord, argument, dissension, or any kind of tumult; in the second, though so many guests were served in so much silver, not one piece was found lost or missing."

Singular indeed, and no modern hostess, where only the most decorated gentlemen and the most décolletées ladies are the guests at massive banquets, could boast of such honesty and decorum. *O tempora! O mores!*

To please the Cardinal and the French Court, Rabelais was constrained to draw up a life horoscope for Monsieur d' Orléans. At his age he had no fear to predict the happiest and the most glorious of careers upon earth. He would certainly not be around to be proven a false prophet. Alas, the princelet died in his cradle some weeks later, ready for immediate dispatch to Heaven and the angels.

The result of the festivities was *La Schiomachie et Festins à Rome au Palais de Mgr. Reveredissime Cardinal du Bellay, pour l'heureuse Naissance de Mgr. d'Orléans, adressés au Cardinal de Guise par M. François Rabelais, Docteur en Médecine.*

This was published in a thirty-page pamphlet by Sebastien Gryphius of Lyons, and it proved the author, man of so many other abilities, also a consummate reporter. But this could have been easily anticipated, since his essays on scientific subjects were precise and objective.

On November 10, 1549, Pope Paul III died. A long struggle for the election of a new pope started at once, French and Spaniards fighting it out bitterly, until at last on February 7, 1550, Cardinal del Monte was duly elected and took the title of Julius III. He was the third pope whom Rabelais had seen. "I have profited little from the sight of them."

And Panurge, when shown a portrait of an ideal pope, adds: "It seems to me that this portrait is faulty as regards our popes, for I have seen them wear a helmet on their heads, and while the whole Christian empire was at peace and quiet, they alone were furiously and very cruelly carrying on wars."

The long confinement of the Conclave, where there was "a great stench," and where at one time there were as many as four hundred persons immured, told severely on Cardinal du Bellay's health. Before midsummer he finally succeeded in being recalled to France, where he could come at his pleasure. He set out, therefore, in the month of July, and in spite of a fall from his horse, which necessitated his continuing the journey on a litter, he reached Paris by slow stages before the end of the month in the company of his faithful physician, François Rabelais.

Rabelais' first thought upon his return was to publish in complete form his *Book Fourth,* which he had in the meantime completed. Conditions, however, were not favorable, and he was reluctant to do it without a royal "privilege." But Cardinal Jean du Bellay was out of favor, and Rabelais angled for a new protector. He found him in the person of Odet de Châtillon (1517-1571).

Odet was the oldest of the Coligny family and at this time a man of thirty-five. At sixteen he had been made cardinal; at seventeen, Archbishop of Toulouse; at twenty-six, Bishop of the rich See of Beauvais. Like his two brothers, he became a Protestant, but was no more a churchman than the high dignitaries and the friends of Rabelais, who remained within the Catholic fold. Odet was a munificent patron of literature and learning and a large proportion of the books published during the reign of Henry II were dedicated to him. He obtained a "privilege" for ten years from the King for Rabelais' new book, granted on August 6, 1550.

The "Privilege" was even more flattering than that granted by Henri's father, François. "Therefore it is that we, inclining freely unto the supplication and request of the said Maître Rabelais, and devoting ourselves to the desired task of entreating him well and favorably in this matter, do accord, permit, and grant, by these presents, that he have the power, by such printers as he shall see fit to cause to be printed and exposed for sale all and every one of the said books and continuation of *Pantagruel,* no less useful than delightful, and we order the suppression of all pirated editions, *corrumpuz, dépravés, et pervertis en plusieurs endroitz* (corrupted, depraved, and perverted in several places)."

Nevertheless Rabelais delayed the publication of his book, for after the severe Edict of Châteaubriand of June 1551 against the Protestants, publication was a dangerous matter. However, on January 28, 1552, the complete *Book Fourth,* containing fifty-two chapters, appeared.

Despite all precautions, the book was pounced upon by the Sorbonne, and the Parliament of Paris prohibited its sale on the first of March. "Whereas the Faculty of Theology has censored a certain evil work, offered for sale under the title of *Book Fourth of Pantagruel,* with the King's "privilege," the court orders that the book-seller shall be forbidden to sell or to show the said book within a period of fourteen days, during which time the Court orders the King's Procter to inform His Majesty about the aforesaid condemnation pronounced upon the book by the said Faculty of Theology, and to send him a copy thereof to be dealt with at his pleasure."

The printer, Michel Fezandat, having been summoned to Court, was forbidden to sell the work on penalty of corporal punishment. After an interval which cannot be determined, the suspension was withdrawn. In the meantime, however, its author was embittered, and the sands of his days scattered.

18

BOOK FOURTH

Of the Heroic Deeds and Sayings
Of the Worthy
PANTAGRUEL
Composed by M. François Rabelais
Doctor of Medicine

Prologue of the Author
To His Benevolent Readers

*M*y good folks, may God save and keep you.
Where are you? I cannot see you. Wait a minute until I straddle my specs. Ah, ha! Fine and
fair is Lent! You've had a good vintage this year. You've
found a never-failing remedy against thirst. But you
yourselves, your wives and children, your families and
relatives, are you all in as good health as you could wish?
That's fine, that's good, that suits me. As for me, I'm
all there. I am, thanks to a little Pantagruelism—and
that, you understand, is a certain cheerfulness of disposition, preserved in spite of all fortuitous circumstances—
very fine and fit and ready to have a little drink, if that
suits you.

In the Gospel we hear that the physician who is
negligent of his own health being reproved with terrible
sarcasm and annihilating bitterness: "Physician, heal
thyself."

In Galen's work, we find:

"He comes to others with his doctor's lore;
Yet he himself is a running sore."

It is hard to have any faith in a physician's ability to look after the health of others, when he is careless of his own health. And that, my gouty friends, is what I found my hope upon. I am firmly convinced that if the good God pleases, you shall obtain the gift of health, seeing that, for the present that is all I ask.

All right then, assuming that you are in good health, take a good cough for yourselves; take also a good triple-sized drink; wiggle your ears for all get-out; and be ready to hear marvels told of our friend, the noble Pantagruel.

In the month of June, on the day of the Feast of Vesta, Pantagruel took leave of good Gargantua, his father, and at an early hour set sail. The flagship was *Thalamege,* and it had on its poop, by way of ensign, a large, commodious bottle, half of smooth and polished silver and half of gold, enameled a carnation red; from which it might readily be deduced that white and red were the colors of these noble travelers, and as an indication that they were on their way to consult the Oracle of the *Holy Bacbuc,* which is the equivalent of *Bottle* in Hebrew.

On the poop of the second ship was reared an antique lantern, fashioned with much fine workmanship of transparent phengites stone, by way of denoting that they were to pass through the Lantern country.

On the fourth day they discovered an island named Medamothi, whose ruler was King Philophane. Pantagruel, Friar John, Panurge, all took a walk in the port, and since a fair was going on, bought many rare and precious things, paintings, tapestries, three young and beautiful unicorns and a tarand, an animal about as large as a bull, who changed colors according to the things which he approached, but whose normal color was that of a jackass. (And perhaps his normal self.)

When Pantagruel and Gargantua desired to have news of each other, they employed as messengers trained pigeons which traveled in one hour the distance boats required three days and three nights.

Father and son exchanged gifts through the good offices of Malicorne, Gargantua's stable-master, who arrived in his brigantine, named *Chelidoine,* while Pantagruel was at the port of Medamothi. The paternal and filial love of these two men was a delight and a model for all. Perhaps Maître Rabelais had dreamed of such a relationship between himself and Théodule, the lovely boy who died at the age of two.

On the fifth day, they discovered a boat which had come from the Lantern country and brought great news to the place. While Pantagruel and the others were engaged in conversation, Panurge got into a scrape with a merchant by the name of Dindenault, who had a flock of sheep on board.

Dindenault insulted him by saying that he looked like a typical cuckold, his Achilles' heel. They nearly came to blows, but were separated by Friar John. Now Panurge was out to take revenge on this impertinent and sarcastic fellow, who like many of Maître Rabelais' characters quoted mythology and Scripture, and thereby considered himself a superior scoundrel to Panurge.

Panurge asked him to sell him one of his sheep, waving a purse filled with new *henricus* in his face, but Dindenault played coy. "Friend and neighbor," he said, "these sheep are issued from the same race which carried Phrixus and Helen across the sea called the Hellespont."

"Sell me one. I shall pay you royally," Panurge persisted.

"You must know that on any field wherever these

sheep piss the wheat grows as if God Himself had pissed there. What's more, from their dung, the physicians of our country cure seventy-eight species of diseases."

Dindenault continued quoting and misquoting, and every now and then called Panurge a cuckold, until finally the owner of the boat warned him: "Sell, if you wish; if you don't wish to, don't annoy the man."

"I sell," the man replied.

Panurge chose a handsome and large sheep bleating desperately, and carried him off. Suddenly, while the merchant continued to make sport of him, Panurge, without retorting, hurled the screaming sheep into the sea. All the other sheep of the flock, bleating as noisily, jumped after him, stampeding and pushing one another into the water, since the sheep, after man, is the most regimented of animals. Save that the sheep, more modest, makes no claim to Divine Revelation and Resurrection, and has no pretension of martyrdom and to glory.

Dindenault, alarmed, tried with all his might to stop them, but in vain. In desperation, he grabbed a big sheep by the nape of the neck, hoping thus to hold him back, but the powerful beast dragged the man into the water. And so sheep and merchant all were drowned.

But Panurge was hardly happy. "It cost me fifty thousand francs, this little pastime," he said. "Let's sail on, the wind is propitious."

And he agreed that vengeance, as the ancient sages taught, is a fruit of the Tree of Bitterness, and the storm of mockery howls in vain at the gate of the deaf ear.

After putting in at a number of exotic ports of call, they passed Pettifoggery, which is a country all blotted and blurred. There they saw gathered some Pettifoggers and some Shysteroos, or writ-servers, fellows capable of anything.

One of the interpreters gave Pantagruel an account of how these people earned their living in a very strange fashion, by taking a good thrashing; and, as a matter of fact, if they went for too long a time without being trounced, they died of hunger—they, their families, and their offspring.

And there appeared Maître François Villon, the poet, who played a trick on the Shysteroos and on the Devil, but whether his shade is angry at Maître Rabelais for making him star in a non too-subtle farce, only they who take walks in the Elysian Fields and gossip about things that once upon a time took place upon earth, know. And whether they care or not, whether they laugh or weep as they recall their life in the flesh, has yet to be revealed.

Now Pantagruel passed the islands of Tohu and Bohu, which in the Hebrew of Genesis means without form and void, and in which he found nothing on fire. For the great Nose-splitter had swallowed all the stoves, saucepans, kettles, earthen pots, drip pans, and frying pans in the country, from lack of windmills, which were his regular diet, and he naturally had a severe case of indigestion. However, he did not die because of the ironware in his guts, but by strangulation from eating a lump of fresh butter at the mouth of a hot oven on the advice of his physicians. This showed, according to Doctor Rabelais, who knew better than all, how perishable life was and how perilous the services of the men of medicine.

The next day, on the right-hand side, they ran into nine transports full of monks, including Jacobins, Jesuits, Capuchins, Hermits, Augustinians, Bernardines, Celestines, Theatins, Egnatins, Amadeans, Franciscans, Carmelites, Minims, and other holy brothers, all of them on their way to the Council to sift the articles of faith against the new heretics.

Panurge was excessively joyful, feeling assured that they would have good luck all that day. Instead, however, a terrific typhoon raised up and suspended mountainous waves from the deep, which, indeed, should have been foreseen, since from time immemorial the presence of men of God always signified evil tidings.

Being a scoundrel, Panurge was inevitably a coward. While all the mariners were busy trying to keep the boats afloat, he ran from poop to stern shouting, praying, moaning. "O God, our Saviour! O my friends! A little vinegar! I'm sweating like Jazus! Here, friends, let me get behind one of those piles! Baa, baa, boo, hoo, hoo! It's all over with me, I can see that! I'm drowning! I'm dying, mates! Boo, boo, hoo, hoo, oo, oo, oo, hoo!"

"I swear," said Friar John, "by the blood, body, belly and head of Christ that if I hear you whimpering just one more time more, you damned cuckold, you, I'll flay you like a seawolf! Holy Christ! Why don't we toss him to the bottom, anyway?"

"Land! Land!" suddenly called out Pantagruel. "I see land! We are not far from port. Courage, children! Look at all the boats which have been sent to save us."

"Ah! Ah!" cried Panurge, "everything is fine! The storm's over. I beg you, permit me to be the first one to disembark. I have some very important business to attend to. Ha, ha, but everything's lovely! I don't fear anything but danger."

The ships of the joyous convoy having been repaired, the men set sail with great good cheer. About midday, they saw from some distance off the Island of Sneaks, where Lentkeeper reigned. Pantagruel would have wished to meet the king, but Xenomenes discouraged him. "All you will find there," he said, "is a big swallower of dried peas, a big lummex of keg-smasher, a big over-grown mole-catcher, a big hay-bundler and half-giant with downy wool and a double tonsure, of Lanternese descent, a flogger of little children, a calcinator of ashes, the father and chief support of physicians, rich in par-dons, indulgences, and stations of the cross, a good Cath-olic, and extremely devout: he weeps three times a day.

And you will never, never find him at a wedding. And now let's head in some other direction. Good-bye, old Lentkeeper."

Towards noon, approaching the Ferocious Island, Pantagruel saw from afar a monstrous whale coming directly towards them noisily, snorting, swelling, and jetting water out of his vast mouth, as if it had been a great river tumbling from some mountain. Panurge, having degenerated into a morbid coward by the will of his Creator, Maître Rabelais, or by his own nature, as is the way between authors and their characters, who are often one another's mortal enemies, began to moan and lament. "He will swallow us all, people and vessels like pills. Let us run away! Let us reach land!"

"Do not fear," Pantagruel tried to console him, "I shall pierce him!"

And peerless hunter that he was, he began to hurl arrows at the great beast, so well aimed that he killed him before he could do any damage, and was taken in tow to port.

Here Pantagruel learned of the long war going on between the Sneaks and the Chitterlings, a stupid and ferocious war similar to the one that Rabelais had witnessed between the faction of his father and that of Gaucher de Sainte-Marthe, when he returned to his "Cow-country, La Devinière," years ago.

The Chitterlings, or Sausages, were properly combatted by cooks, Friar John drawing them up for battle. In imitation of the Trojan Horse, he had the engineers construct a huge sow and the cooks entered it. The Chitterlings attacked, but Friar John with a big iron bar mowed them down like flies. The entire Chitterlingish race would have been exterminated by these culinary troops, had God's hand not interfered.

Why had He not interfered at the beginning of the war, and indeed why had He not interfered at the beginning of all wars, to bring peace among men? These were grave questions whose answers could only be found in the Labyrinth of the Theologians, but no one venturing to enter it has ever managed to find his way out. No Ariadne, daughter of Reason, has ever offered him a thread.

Two days later they arrived in the Island of Rauch, which in the tongue of the Teutons means Fume, where the state of the people was the strangest imaginable. They lived only by wind. They ate nothing but wind. In their houses they had nothing except weathercocks. In their gardens they only planted three species of anemones. The rich fed on windmills. They all died of hydrophobia, swollen; their souls, leaving via their arses —perhaps the usual exit of all souls, for what self-respecting soul would care to leave by the mouth, that cave of lies?

The next morning they reached the Isle of the Popefiggers, who had originally been known as Protestants, and whose inhabitants formerly were rich and happy. Now they were poor and unhappy, and subjects of the Papamaniacs.

And this is how it came about. One day during the great feast in Papamania, one of the watchers, upon seeing the portrait of the Pope being carried aloft in the parade, shook his fist at it. To avenge this insult, the Papamaniacs armed themselves quietly, and a few days later surprised, sacked and ruined the whole island and put all men to the sword. They spared the women and the children, but they were made slaves of the Papamaniacs, and the name of Popefiggers was imposed upon them, because they had waved a fist at the papal portrait.

Since that time, the poor people had not prospered. Every year there was hail, tempest, hunger, and every kind of misfortune, as the eternal punishment for the sin their ancestors had committed.

Seeing the misery and calamity of these people, the voyagers did not wish to go any further, for the misfortune of others reminds us of what may be in store for us, too, and we must live in the glorious shadow of the Fata Morgana of the Future. We are in perpetual transit and time burns the bridges behind us, while the future is the creation of our despair.

The voyagers only entered a little chapel, in ruins and desolation, very near the port, took some holy water and recommended themselves to God. Pantagruel in a magnanimous gesture left the poor people 18,000 gold royaux.

From there Pantagruel and his company sailed for Papimania, where the Decretals of the Church were exposed in all their crudeness, and Maître François Rabelais, Medicus, flayed the Papacy by the scalpel of sarcasm and the dagger of laughter. That the institution still exists and flourishes is proof that the saying, "The pen is mightier than the sword," is but the illusion and the despair of the ink dwellers.

The waters carry almost all that the writers have ever penned on paper and on parchment, and carved on wood and on stone, yet they weigh not one drop more, nor are they purified. "Be admonished: of making many books there is no end; and much study is a weariness of the flesh."

Pantagruel now disembarked at a most wonderful island—wonderful both because of its situation and of its governor, Sir Gaster, otherwise Sir Belly, Master of all the arts. To this knightly King it is our duty to do reverence, swear obedience, and show honor; for he is imperious, rigorous, round, hard to please, inflexible. He cannot be made to believe anything, he cannot be shown anything or be persuaded of anything, for the reason that he does not hear a thing.

He speaks only by signs, but these signs are obeyed by all the world more quickly than are the edicts of praetors and the commands of kings; he permits no delay, no tarrying whatsoever in connection with the summonses. At Sir Gaster's command all the heavens tremble and the earth shakes. And his command is: Do what you must do, without delay, or die.

Into whatever company he may go, there can be no discussion there of first rank or preference; for he always goes before all others, even though they be kings, emperors, or the Pope himself. To serve him all the world is busy, all the world labors; and as a recompense he does this for all the world: he invents for it all the arts, all machines, all trades, all implements, and all refinements. He even teaches the brute beasts arts that have been denied them by Nature. Crows, jays, popinjays, starlings. He makes poets of them all; and of the magpies, he makes poetesses, teaching them to speak and sing in the tongue of human beings. *And all for the guts.*

Eagles, gerfalcons, falcons, sakers, lanners, goshawks, sparrowhawks, merlins, wild birds, migratory birds, flying birds, birds of prey, savage birds—he domesticates and tames them all, in such a manner that, turning them loose in the heavens when he sees fit and leaving them free to fly as high as he wishes, holding them there suspended in their wandering and hovering flight while they flirt with him and pay court from above the clouds, he is still able suddenly to bring them down to earth. *And all for the guts.*

Elephants, lions, rhinoceroses, bears, horses, dogs—he makes them all hop and skip and dance, fight, swim, hide themselves, and fetch and carry for him, taking what he would have them take. *And all for the guts.*

Fishes—both sea fish and fresh-water ones—whales and marine monsters—he causes them all to leap up from the lowest depths; he hurls the wolves out of the forests, the bears from their rocks, foxes out of their holes, and serpents out of the earth. *And all for the guts.*

The short of it is: he is so enormous that, in his fury, he eats everything, beasts and men. *And all for the guts.*

When Penia, otherwise known as Poverty, his queen-regent takes the war path, wherever she may go, all parliaments are closed, all decrees are mute, and all statutes vain. For she is subject to no law, but is exempt from all. Everybody, everywhere, flees her approach, preferring to run the risk of shipwrecks at sea or to pass through fire, over mountains, or through the depths of abysses, to being apprehended by her.

Sir Gaster invented agriculture and the blacksmith's art, to enable him to cultivate the earth so that it might produce grain for him. He invented the art of war and of arms in order to defend his grain, and invented medicine and the requisite mathematical sciences to preserve his grain in safety for a number of centuries and to put it beyond the reach of atmospheric disasters, the depredations of brute beasts, and the thieving of brigands.

He invented water mills, windmills, hand mills, and a myriad other contrivances to grind his grain and reduce it to flour; invented leaven to ferment the dough and salt to give it flavor. He also invented fire to bake with and clocks and dials to mark the time that his bread, which is the creature of grain, took in baking.

Displaying further a vast degree of inventiveness, he proceeded to mix two species of animals, asses and mares, in order to produce a third species, which we call mules. He also invented carts and chariots to haul his grain more conveniently.

If sea or rivers stood in the way of transportation, he invented boats, galleys, and ships in order to be able to travel and bring grain from barbarous, unknown, and widely separated lands. He invented the art of building cities, strongholds, and castles, where he might store the grain and keep it in safety. He invented cannons, ser-pentines, culverins, big-gauge guns and basilisks, hurling iron, lead, and bronze bullets weighing more than great anvils. And one single basilisk shot is more horrible, more frightful, more diabolic, and murders, mangles, and wipes out more people, and in general perturbs the human senses, as well as demolishing more walls than a hundred thunderbolts.

There were the myriad myriad Gastrolates, who wor-shiped and sacrificed only to Gaster, the greatest of all the gods, although Gaster himself confessed that he was not a god, but a poor, sickly, vile creature. And he sent his worshipers to his chamberpot to see, consider, phi-losophize and contemplate what divinity they discovered in his fecal matter. But this only excited greater venera-tion to see how humble a great divinity could be. And they said that all gods were humble, only their repre-sentatives were haughty. And they further said that while gods had stables for their homes, their representa-tives had palaces.

The voyagers now reached the Isle of Ganabim, which in Hebrew means Thieves and Rascals, although it re-sembled strongly Mount Parnassus. Perhaps, indeed, many a vulgar robber of poetic laurels sat enthroned there, while those of princely blood, ragged beggars, when alive called in vain to the gods for justice, and when dead rotted, forsaken in their graves. They were not forgotten, for they had never been remembered. Men have corrupted the gods, and there is as much injustice in Heaven as upon earth.

At the word "Robbers," Panurge was scared out of his wits, and he implored Pantagruel not to land on that island. So overwhelmed was he that he mistook a cat for the devil and defecated all over himself. Friar John, who had been teasing Panurge all the time, tightened his nos-trils and pointed at him in disgust. Pantagruel, as always the unperturbed prince, said: "For God's sake, Panurge, go, take a bath and put on a clean shirt." Polite, yet hardly the anxious words of one who had vowed eternal friendship. But time is the sea in which all passions are extinguished.

After some more foolish remarks, Panurge, as if to blow away all stench of his body and the stench of dead time, called out: "*Buvons!* Let us drink!" And upon that word, like a hammer blow, *Book Fourth*—that strange, incomparable tour of the world of the most worthy François Rabelais, Doctor of Medicine, ends. And with it his last book published during his lifetime.

Panurge, changed into a stinking coward, had not been made a cuckold for the very good reason that he had not found a wife. Indeed, he and his companions had completely forgotten the grand objective of their great voyage, and never even mentioned it.

And it was a great voyage in the style of the day, showing once more Rabelais a true man of the Renaissance, identified with all the momentous projects of his time, well-versed in its problems, master of terminology without which man is lost in the wilderness of things.

Only two years or so before his birth, the Great Admiral crossed the Atlantic; in 1497 Vasco da Gama reached India by the Cape of Good Hope; in 1513 Vasco Nuñez de Balboa saw "the Pacific stretch at his feet"; in 1521 Ferdinand de Magellan sailed through the straits that later bore his name; in 1534 Jacques Cartier sailed through the Strait of Belle Isle, reached the Gulf of St. Lawrence, and navigated it as far as Montreal.

Many a valiant sailor dreamed of that fabulous Northwest Passage—John Davis, Walter Raleigh, Henry Hudson, Sir Francis Drake—the sea passage from the Atlantic to the Pacific through the Arctic ocean north of Canada and Alaska. Sir John Franklin (1786-1847),

British naval officer, discovered it on his last expedition, in which he and his entire party died of exposure and starvation, their bodies found in 1880 by Lieutenant Schwatka. However, it proved impracticable for commercial navigation.

Many were the books recording these voyages, mingling factual observations with extravagant interpretations. One of the most important, published in 1532, was *Novus Orbis*—The New World—by Johann Huttich, with an introduction by the Hebrew scholar and mathematician, Sebastian Münster (1489-1552), author of *Cosmographia Universa,* and disciple of Elias Levita. He also published more than one Hebrew grammar and edited the Hebrew Bible in two volumes, accompanied by a new Latin translation.

These books and the *True History* by Lucian were the inspirations of Rabelais, but he added his own inimitable sense of humor (often too peppered with scatology), and his castigation with laughter and scorn of the follies and cruelties of his generation, and in particular those of the Roman Church, which he considered the worst. He succeeded, as all artists succeed, only partially, yet even so, it was the best writing of the period by any Frenchman.

19

"DIABOLE"—A WORTHY CURÉ—
DISAPPEARANCE

*I*n the year 1549, a monk of the monastery of Fon-
tevrault, by the name of Gabriel de Puy-Herbault—
in Latin Putherbus—wrote a treatise entitled *The-
otimus, Sive de Tollendis et Expurgandis Malis Libris*
(On the Suppression and Expurgation of Evil Books)
in which he attacked François Rabelais, accusing him of
impiety, disbelief, Calvinism. "Would to God," he cried,
"that he were in Geneva, he and his Pantagruelism, if he
is still alive, for at the beginning of this reign of Henry
II, he followed the rabble of the dismissed Cardinals
relegated to Rome.

"All the more wicked is he, for the reason that he is
learned, being one who makes so little of God and divine
things, that with the exception of Impudence and Abuse,
those goddesses to whom the Athenians sacrificed upon
their altars, it would seem that he does not recognize any
religion whatsoever. Rabelais is as dangerous on account
of his impiety as he is by reason of the public scandal
which his books cause.

"He is possessed of neither the fear of God nor the
respect for men, but tramples under foot and turns into
ridicule all things human and divine. More than once
have I deplored the fate of a man who brings to his
damnation that erudition with which he is endowed."

Unwillingly, unwittingly, the monk praises Rabelais'

198

genius, for within his books can be found *"une celeste et impréciable drogue*—the soundest clue to the labyrinthine mysteries of morality and philosophy—common sense, with the most ordinary human kindliness and generosity to get us wisely, humanly and humbly through this mad world, between man and man and race and race."

But the monk, not satisfied to impugn atheism and heresy, painted Rabelais also as a drunkard, a glutton, a cynic—a portrait which for a very long time was considered factual and still lingers in the minds of those who know him only by the adjective "Rabelaisian."

Putherbus was supported in his attack by the court poet Charles de Sainte-Marthe, son of Gaucher de Sainte-Marthe, the ancient enemy of Antoine Rabelais, father of François. Thus had the feud which had inspired the great and ludicrous battle in *Gargantua* come back to torture the author in his declining years. It would seem that it is as dangerous to laugh in the wind as to spit in it, and the acid we splash at the world burns our own faces.

"In Greek," Rabelais writes, "calumny is called *diabole*. How detestable before God and the angels is this vice, calumny, by which the devils are distinguished and named!"

Yet, despite all, when Rabelais returned to France from Rome, not only was he not annoyed, but being already Curé of St. Christophe-du-Jambet in the diocese of Mans, he was also appointed Curé de Meudon, near Paris. According to the testimony of his earliest biographer, the poet Guillaume Colletet (1598-1650), and later investigations, Rabelais, the unbeliever, fulfilled the duties of his curacy with great dignity and devotion, for he was an honorable man and generous and kindly in his relations with people. Indeed, that was the sum total of his religion. The dogmas of the Church being largely meaningless to him, he could accept them gracefully when necessary. He had not enough faith to sin against the faith. What he had at heart was the interest of his country and its sovereign without papal interference, and without the flow of the French gold to the Roman coffers.

"His house at Meudon, while closed to women, was open to scholars with whom he loved to converse. He detested ignorance, especially in ecclesiastics, and when characterizing illiterate priests, he would recover the satirical verve of the author of Pantagruel. For the rest, these were the only people towards whom he was lacking in charity. The poor were always certain to receive help from his purse. His integrity was so great that he was never known to fail to keep his word with anybody. His medical knowledge had rendered him doubly useful to his parish. He was very punctilious in the care of his flock and taught the plain-song, of which he was master, to the children.

"The Curé of Meudon filled his curacy with all the sincerity, all the kindness and all the charity expected of a man who was anxious to fulfill his duty. At least, neither by tradition, nor otherwise, can we find any complaint lodged against his morals or his care of the flock. On the contrary, there is every evidence that his flock was very much pleased with him, as may be inferred from certain letters, which he wrote to some friends, still preserved, where he says, among other things, that he has good and pious parishioners in the persons of *Monsieur et Madame de Guise* (the Duke and the Cardinal de Guise had just bought the castle of Meudon), proof of the great care with which he discharged his duty and won the affection of those whose spiritual direction had been entrusted to him by his Bishop, Eustache du Bellay, nephew of Cardinal Jean."

Why, when at last he had two "livings," financial security, and honorable employment, did François Rabe-

lais relinquish all and take to his heels? Was it his ancient irresistible urge to wander, a nomad in search of
knowledge and excitement? Did he suffer from accidie—
that creeping languor, fatigue and temporary paralysis
of the spirit? Or was he in the throes of a mortal physical illness, and preferred to hide from the eyes of those
who knew him, and who would offer preposterous pity?

We only know that in the Archives of the Secretariat
of the Bishop of Paris was his formal resignation of
the Curés of Jambet and Meudon, on the 9th of January,
1552. But no comment by his superior, no commendations, no regrets. Not one paragraph. Not one line. Nothing. Nothing more. Franciscus Rabelaeus, Medicus, was,
to all intents and purposes, no more.

A wandering scholar by the name of Denys Lambin
(1516-1572), learned at Lyons at the end of the month
of November, 1552, that Rabelais had been imprisoned
and chained. When he arrived in Paris in December,
Lambin was sufficiently interested about "the fate of the
clown, who invented Pantagruelism," to make inquiries,
and wrote to his friend, Henri Estienne, that the rumor
had been false. More than that, however, he could not
discover.

And the only thing we know is that Rabelais died in a
house in Paris on Rue des Jardins and was buried either
in the cemetery proper under a tree, "which stood for
many, many years," or in the nave itself of St. Paul's
Church, situated near the Bastille, at the time a quarter
neither fashionable nor sanitary, and long since vanished.

His death presumably occurred within the last six
months of the year 1553, perhaps on April 9, judged
according to the publication of a volume of poems at
Poitiers in May, 1554, by Jacques Tahureau de la Mans
—*Premières Poésies,* in which appeared the first epitaph:
RABELAIS TREPASSE—RABELAIS DEAD:

Ce docte nez Rabelays, qui picquoyt
Les plus piquans, dort soubz la lame icy
Et de ceux mêsmes en mourant se moquoit
Qui de sa mort prenoyent quelque soucy.

(This learned Rabelais who stung even the most stinging ones, sleeps under this stone. And in dying he mocked even those who were most concerned over his death.)

At the same time, a learned physician of Loudon, Pierre Boulanger, who had known Rabelais, wrote in Latin verse, as was the custom, a second epitaph.

"Beneath this stone sleeps the most excellent of laughing men. Our descendants will seek out the kind of man he was, for all who lived in his time well know who he was; everyone knew him, and more than any other, he was dear to all. Perhaps they will believe that he was a buffoon, a clown, who by dint of his jokes earned a good meal. No, no, he was not a buffoon, nor a public clown. But, with his exquisite and penetrating genius, he mocked at the human race, at its insensate desires and the credulity of its hopes.

"Undisturbed about his fate, he led a happy life; the winds always blew in his favor. Yet, no more learned man could be found, when, forgetting his jokes, he was pleased to talk seriously, and to play a serious part. Never did any Senator with threatening brow and severe and melancholy glance, sit more easily upon his lofty seat. A large and difficult question had only to be propounded and to require great skill and knowledge for its solution and you would have thought that large subjects were open to him alone and to him only were the secrets of Nature revealed.

"With what eloquence he could adorn whatever he was pleased to say, to the admiration of all whom his biting pleasantries and his usual witticisms had led to believe that this joker was nothing of a scholar! He knew everything that Greece and Rome produced, but like a new Democritus, he laughed at the vain fears and the desires of the common people and of princes, at their frivolous cares and at the anxious labors of this brief life in which is consumed all the time that a benevolent divinity is willing to grant us."

There was also Antoine de Báíf (1532-1589), Venetian by birth, a poet of the *Pléiade,* who wrote:

> *O Pluton, Rabelais reçoy!*
> *Afin que toi qui es le roy*
> *De ceux qui ne rit jamais,*
> *Tu aies un rieur désormais.*

(O Pluto, welcome Rabelais, so that you, King of the Mirthless, may possess one jester henceforth!)

And the Latin epitaph by Joachim du Bellay (1522-1560), one of the most remarkable of the *Pléiade* poets:

> *Fuit ars mihi cura medendi,*
> *Maxima ridenda sed mihi cura fuit,*
> *Tu quoque non lacrymas sed risum hic solve, viator,*
> *Si gratus nostris manibus esse cupis.*

(The cult of healing was my concern; innately more the cult of mirth. If you wish to please my shade, traveler, burst not into tears, but into laughter.)

But the *coup de grâce* was delivered by Pierre de Ronsard (1524-1585), "Prince of Poets." Of a noble family and attached to the royal house, Ronsard's promising diplomatic career was cut short by an attack of deafness, which no physician could cure, and he determined to devote himself to letters.

His poetry had an overwhelming success and his prosperity was unbroken. He received grants and endowments not only from his own sovereign, but from many others, including Elizabeth of England and Mary, Queen of Scots.

However, his last years were filled with sorrow, not only by the death of most of his friends, but by constant and increasing ill health.

He was the chief member of the poetic group of the *Pléiade,* which sought to improve the French language and literature by the enthusiastic imitation of the classics. Ronsard shows eminently the two great attractions of the sixteenth-century poetry—magnificence of language and imagery and graceful variety of meter.

Ronsard painted François Rabelais after the Puij-Herbault portrait and in the form of Anacreontics, named for the Greek poet, Anacreon (born 560 B.C.), who devoted himself to the "triple worship," Muses, Wine and Love, vulgarized by the Teutons in later centuries into *Wein, Weib und Gesang.* It was a form *à la mode* during the sixteenth and seventeenth centuries in France and in England, where William Oldys (1696-1761) was its chief exponent with *To a Fly,* as a typical example:

> Busy, curious, thirsty fly,
> Drink with me, and drink as I,
> Freely welcome to my cup,
> Couldst thou sip and sip it up,
> Make the most of life you may;
> Life is short and wears away.

Epitaphe À François Rabelais par Pierre Ronsard

> *Jamais le soleil ne l'a vu,*
> *Tant fût-il matin, qu'il n'eût bu,*
> *Et jamais au soir, la nuit noire*
> *Tant fût tard, ne l'a vu sans boire. . . .*
> *O toi, quiconque sois, qui passes,*
> *Sur son fosses répands des tasses,*
> *Répands du bril et des flacons,*
> *Des cervelas et des jambons. . . .*

(Never did the sun see him, however early, without his drinking; and never in the evening or at black night, however late, was he seen without drinking. O thou, whoever thou might be, who passes by, upon his grave spread cups and flagons, sausages and hams. . . .)

And again, Ronsard spoke of Rabelais as wallowing in the grass, drunk and half-drunk, "*sans nulle honte comme une grenouille, en la fange*" (without any shame like a frog in the mud).

And what was Pantagruelism, therefore Rabelaisism?

> *C'est du bon temps joyeusement user,*
> *Peu lire ès doctes écritures,*
> *Sans remords prendre ses ébats,*
> *N'avoir procès, ne noise, ne débats,*
> *Chercher souvent la gente bachelette,*
> *Boire et manger, rire et chanter d'autant,*
> *Sans cure avoir, ne soin de demeurant.*

(It is to make a joyous use of fair weather, to read little in the learned writings, to take one's diversions without remorse, to have no lawsuits, quarrels and disputes, to seek often the gentle maid, to drink and eat, to laugh and to sing a great deal, without a care or tie.)

Pierre de Ronsard was thirty years old when François Rabelais died at twice that age, and perhaps the two men had never met, although there were stories that they had met in Rome, quarreled over the *Pléiade,* and Rabelais satirizing its classical tendencies in the episode of the Limousin scholar. Therefore, after his death, Ronsard avenged himself by a libelous epitaph.

However, the allusions to the *Pléiade* date from a time when Ronsard was only a boy, and it was not until much later that Bernier told the story borrowed from an earlier writer, Geoffroy Tory, who had heard it rumored. But the notion traveled athwart the generations.

There was, to be sure, no reason for Ronsard to have been an admirer of Rabelais. They belonged to totally different literary schools and had completely different trainings and careers. Moreover, Rabelais never extricated himself from the Middle Ages and its crudities, while Ronsard was a man of the chivalrous world with its superficialities as well as its elegancies. But there is no evidence whatsoever that they had been enemies, or that Ronsard wished to avenge himself for some wrong done him personally or his school of poetry.

Why, then, did Ronsard write about the old Master as he did? Did he mean to besmirch him? Did he mean to hold him up to ridicule? Was it all a bit of spoofing? Was it a show of virtuosity? Did he wish to prove that if he so willed, he, too, could write in the vein of the author of *Pantagruel* and evoke laughter? Did he, perhaps, really mean to compliment Rabelais by taking the trouble of writing an epitaph?

Whatever the poet's purpose, whether good or evil, or both, the interpretation was the mutilation of character of an honorable man, and the mistinterpretation of a masterpiece. And because it was the work of a Prince of Poetry, it lasted for so long, and may never die.

It was 1562. Nine years had passed since Rabelais' demise, and there were no more epitaphs, and it seemed as if the good Doctor would be allowed to rest in peace wherever they had laid him—at least for a while. But all of a sudden, there appeared a thin octavo volume of thirty-two leaves and fifteen chapters, without the name of printer, publisher or place of publication, entitled *L'Isle Sonnante* (The Ringing Island) by Maître *François Rabelais,* with the disconcerting stanza of four lines, signed *Nature Quite,* perhaps an anagram on the name of Jean Turquet:

> Is Rabelais dead? A book see yet again?
> His better part with life is still aglow,
> Another of his writings to bestow,
> Which make him live immortal among men.

The question of Rabelais' death was rhetorical, but the author of the book has been in question ever since the seventeenth century. Meanwhile, two years later appeared another volume containing forty-seven chapters, which have remained the definitive *Book Fifth,* and which in time became the battleground for scholarly disputants as to its authenticity.

The opponents of the book's authorship relied on the testimony of one, Louis Guyon, who in 1604 declared that *Book Fifth* had been made years after Rabelais' death by an author whom he knew, and who was not a doctor, but an *"écolier de Valence";* on the fact that the antimonastic, anti-Catholic polemic was overaccentuated; that some of the parts were apparently replicas of rough drafts already appearing in the previous books; that some allusions were manifestly posterior to even the furthest date which could be assigned to Rabelais.

But the conflict finally subsided, and now the general opinion is that the book was indeed written by François Rabelais, but never revised by him, and that the editors, as editors everywhere and always, meddled seriously with the manuscript, considering it their duty to "improve" upon the style, to add some of their own stuff, and in general to mutilate it. However, all in all, the book deserves to make part of the monumental work of the Master, and has so been used in all of the modern editions.

Book Fifth relates the continuation and end of the journey of Pantagruel and his companions in search of the Oracle of the Holy Bottle.

20

BOOK FIFTH AND LAST

OF THE HEROIC DEEDS AND SAYINGS
of the
WORTHY PANTAGRUEL
COMPOSED

by

M. François Rabelais
Doctor of Medicine

*O*n the fourth day of the voyage, they saw land and the pilot said that it was *"L'Isle Sonnante"* (The Ringing Island). In fact, they heard the continuous noise of all kinds of bells ringing. They had to fast for four days, however, before they were allowed to land, a terrible experience, particularly for Panurge.

A little old man named Albian Camar, Maître Aeditue, or Sacristan, welcomed them and became their guide. He showed them that the Island was inhabited solely by birds, which dwelt in cages, large and beautiful, and marvelously built. The birds within them were equally large and handsome, resembling the human beings the voyagers had left at home. They ate and drank like men, digested like men, defecated like men, slept and snored like men. In short, at first sight you would have taken them for men, nevertheless they were not. Their plumage also made the voyagers wonder. Some were all white; others all black; others all gray; others half white and half black; others still, all red, and half white and blue.

The males were named Clerghawks, Monkhawks, Priesthawks, Abbothawks, Bishhawks, Cardinhawks and Popehawk, the only one of his species. The females were named Clergkites, Nunkites, Priestkites, Bishkites, Cardinkites, Popekite.

These birds gave birth to one another, but not by carnal copulation, but by Holy Ghosts.

Friar John said: "These birds neither toil nor cultivate the land; their whole occupation is to frolic, warble and sing. From what country does this horn of abundance come, this store of so many good things and dainty bits?"

"From all over the world, except some countries of the Northern regions," replied Aeditue.

On the third day, the voyagers were allowed to see the Popehawk in his cage, where he sat, his feathers drooping, staring about him, attended by a brace of little Cardinhawks and six lusty, fusty Bishhawks. Panurge stared at him, examining exactly his figure, his size, his motions. Then in a loud voice he said: "A curse light on the hatcher of this ill bird! Upon my word this is a filthy whoophooper!"

"Speak low," warned Aeditue, "for he has ears. If he should hear you blaspheme thus, good people, you are lost. Do you see in this cage a basin? From that he will draw out thunder and lightning, the devil, and the tempest, by which in one moment you will be engulfed a hundred feet under the earth."

Angered, Panurge was about to hurl a stone at one of the Bishhawks. He was warned by the guide not to dare do it. "Strike, poison, kill and murder all the kings and princes in the world, by treachery or how you will, and as soon as you would; unsettle the angels from their cockloft; Popehawk will pardon you all this. But never be so mad as to meddle with these Sacred Birds, as much as you love the profit, welfare and life, not only of your-

self and your friends and relations alive or dead, but
also of those that may be born after the thousandth
generation."

"Truly, truly, this rascally monastic vermin all over
the world mind nothing but their guts and are as ravenous as any kites," said Panurge. "Let's drink!"

"Now you are talking!" said Aeditue. "Speaking thus,
you will never be a heretic."

"It's better to eat and to banquet," added Panurge.

And Friar John said: "You are right. Seeing these
devils of birds, we do nothing but blaspheme. Emptying
our bottles we do nothing but praise God. Let's drink!
O fine word!"

But Pantagruel and his crew had no need to travel
to the "Ringing Island" to discover the truth about these
strange birds. Cardinal Lorraine, a highly Orthodox
Churchman, wrote in October, 1548: "Bishops are ignorant and uncharitable; a large number of priests are
worthless; canons refuse to pay their bishops and monks
their abbots; benefices are held by absentees at the Papal
Court, who out of the yearly income of 30 or 40 crowns
take 25, and leave the rest to some poor curé."

They visited a variety of islands and reached the *Isle
des Chats Fourrés* (Furred Cats) ruled by Archduke
Grippeminaud—Hypocrite. The Furred Cats—Priest-
cats and Lawcats—horrible and frightening creatures.
They grabbed everything, devoured everything, burned,
beheaded, murdered, imprisoned, ruined everything.
They called vice virtue, evil good, treason fidelity, and
lived by corruption. After having destroyed and devoured their castles, domains, estates, possessions, revenues, they sought blood and souls in the next world.

It was a disagreeable visit for the voyagers, and only
after many difficulties and bribery were they allowed to
leave the Island.

They arrived at the Port of Mathéotecine, which

means Vain Science, and desired to pay their respects
to Queen Quintessence, as well as to visit the celebrated
Kingdom of Entelechia, or Perfection.

Queen Quintessence, young at the age of at least 1,800
years, cured the sick by playing pieces on the organ,
different selections for various diseases, even as in the
Christian world, kings, by simply placing their hands
upon the heads of their subjects, cured them of the scro-
fula, fever, and the holy illness.

Among the cures was one which without baths, without
milk, without any drugs, helped the emaciated and the
atrophied, merely by making them monks for three
months; if they were not fattened by their monastic sojourn, neither art nor Nature could ever do it.

Many were the marvels the voyagers saw performed
in the Kingdom of Entelechia, most of them preposterous, but always barbed with sarcasm against the ways
and manners of the men of the Western World, and in
particular the clergy and the advocates.

They continued their journey, and the pilot discovered
a more beautiful and more delightful island than all the
others. Within it there was the country of Satin, so renowned among the pages of the Court. The trees and
the tall grasses never lost either their flowers or their
leaves, which were of velvet and of damask. The birds
and the beasts were made of tapestry.

After having enjoyed the beautiful country of Satin,
Pantagruel said: "I have fed my eyes here for a long
while, and now my stomach is raging with hunger."

And as they went in search of food, they heard a
strident noise as if women were washing their clothes at
the mills of Bazacle, near Toulouse.

Without waiting any longer they betook themselves
to the place where they saw a little, hunchbacked, misshapen, and monstrous old man. He was called Ouï-Dire
—Hearsay. He had his mouth slit open right to his ears,

and within his throat he had seven tongues, and each tongue slit into seven parts. However this might be, he spoke with all seven together, on different subjects, in different languages; also he had over his head and the rest of his body as many ears as Argus formerly had eyes; besides which, he was blind and palsied in his legs.

Around him they saw a vast number of men and women listening attentively, and amongst the group, they recognized some who cut a fine figure, and particularly one who had a *mappa mundi,* explaining it to them minutely in little aphorisms. Thus they became learned clerks in no time, and spoke elegantly and with good memory about a multitude of prodigious things, for the knowledge of a hundredth part of which a man's whole lifetime would not have sufficed—of the Pyramids of the Nile, of Babylon, of the Troglodytes, of the Hymantopodes, of the Blemmyae, of the Pygmies, of the Cannibals, of the Hyperborean Mountains, of the Aegipans, and of all the devils, and of all this by *Hearsay.* . . . And there were travelers and writers on geography who were hidden behind a piece of tapestry, stealthily writing fine stuff, and all by *Hearsay.*

Pantagruel and his men were given bread, and they drank from their barrels as much as they wished. Then they were warned that if they wished to succeed at the houses of the great noblemen, they must be very sparing with the truth. They thanked them for their good advice, and left.

At last they arrived at the Land of Lanterns and the desired Island where dwelt the Oracle of the Holy Bottle.

The approach to the Temple was through a large vineyard. At the bottom of the staircase they found a portal on the front of which was written in Greek, in letters of purest gold: *"En oino aletheia"*—In wine there is truth.

The venerable priestess of the Temple, Bacbuc, ordered her servants to bring goblets of gold, silver, porce-
lain and crystal, filled with wine, and invited the travelers
to drink. "Drink," she said, "once, twice and three times
again, changing your fancy each time, and you will find
the taste, savor and liquor, such as you shall have fan-
cied."

And so they did, and so it proved.

Then Bacbuc asked: "Who among you wishes to have
the word from the Bottle?"

"I, your humble servant," said Panurge.

Thereupon he was wrapt up in a green gaberdine and
otherwise solemnly prepared for the initiation of the
mysteries. He was led to a circular chapel, in the middle
of which was a fountain of fine alabaster full of clear
water. Half immersed in the water was the Sacred Bottle
of pure and beautiful crystal, oval-shaped.

Panurge was made to turn nine times around the fountain, do three beautiful little jumps, strike his arse seven
times against the ground, while the priestess was saying
in Etruscan conjurations and reading in a book of rituals
held for her by one of her mystagogues, the servant of
the mysteries.

Bacbuc, the noble pontifess, made Panurge kiss the
rim of the fountain, and ordered him to dance three short
dances in honor of Bacchus. Then she ordered him to sit
between two stools placed there for the purpose, his arse
upon the ground, and she drew forth a huge silver book
in the form of a breviary, bade Panurge open his mouth
and sing the Baccich song:

> *O Bouteille*
> *Pleine toute*
> *De mystères,*
> *Je t'escoute.*
> *Ne diffères,*

Et le mot profères
Aquel pend mon coeur.
(O Bottle! Whose mysterious Deep
Does all the secrets keep,
With attentive ear I wait,
Ease my mind and speak my fate.)

And out of the Sacred Bottle issued the word: *"Trinc!"*

"Is this all that is meant by the answer of the Bottle?" Panurge, perplexed, asked.

And Bacbuc answered: "Nothing more. *Trinc* is a Panompean word, that is, a word used and understood and celebrated by all nations, and signifies: *Drink.* I don't say drinking, taking that word singly and absolutely in the strictest sense. No, beasts might then put in for a share. I mean drinking cool, delicious wine. For you must know, my beloved, that by wine we become divine; neither can there be a surer argument, or less deceitful divination. Your academics assert the same when they make the etymology of wine, which the Greeks call *oinos,* from *vis,* strength, virtue and power; for it is in its power to fill the soul with all truth, learning and philosophy."

Panurge got no further definite answer to his problem of marriage. Nevertheless he believed that the Holy Bottle had solved it. "Ere long I shall be wedded!" he exclaimed.

Bacbuc gave the voyagers three bottles, and said: "Go, my friends, under the protection of that intellectual Sphere which we call God, whose center is everywhere and circumference nowhere."

And they saw exquisitely engraved upon the door of the Temple, two tablets—one in ancient Latin letters, the iambic verse: *Ducunt volentem fata, nolentem trahunt."* (Fates lead him who consents; pull him who refuses.) The other in French, in capital letters: *"TOUTES CHOSES SE MEUVENT A LEUR FIN."* (ALL THINGS PROCEED TOWARD THEIR END.)

AGATHE TYCHE!
GOOD LUCK TO US ALL!